John Webster, Renaissance Dramatist

John Webster, Renaissance Dramatist

David Coleman

Edinburgh University Press

© David Coleman, 2010

Edinburgh University Press Ltd
22 George Square, Edinburgh

www.euppublishing.com

Typeset in 11.5/13 Monotype Ehrhardt
by Servis Filmsetting Ltd, Stockport, Cheshire, and
printed and bound in Great Britain by
CPI Antony Rowe, Chippenham and Eastbourne

A CIP record for this book is available from the British Library

ISBN 978 0 7486 3464 4 (hardback)
ISBN 978 0 7486 3465 1 (paperback)

Contents

Acknowledgements

Thanks are due to Ewan Fernie, for the initial suggestion that I might write a book on Webster, and to Sean McEvoy, who has been a generous and perceptive editor throughout the writing process. I would also like to thank Jackie Jones and her colleagues at Edinburgh University Press for their professionalism and efficiency. Finally, thanks, as always, to Mary, Niamh, Sophie and Kate.

Chronology

	Plays and playwrights	Theatre and politics
1564	Shakespeare born Marlowe born	
1570		Queen Elizabeth excommunicated by Pope Pius V
1572	Jonson born	Bartholomew's Eve Massacre in France
1576		James Burbage opens The Theatre
1578	Webster born (?)	
1580	Middleton born	Last performance of miracle plays at Coventry
1587	Kyd *The Spanish Tragedy* Marlowe *Tamburlaine*	Mary Queen of Scots executed. Rose Theatre opens
1588	Marlowe *Dr Faustus*	Defeat of Spanish Armada
1589	Marlowe *The Jew of Malta*	
1592	Marlowe *Edward II* Marlowe *Massacre at Paris* Shakespeare *Richard III*	Azores expedition

	Plays and playwrights	Theatre and politics
1593	Marlowe killed Shakespeare *The Taming of the Shrew*	
1594	Shakespeare *Titus Andronicus*	First of four bad harvests
1595	Shakespeare *Richard II*	Spanish raids on Cornwall. O'Neill's revolt in Ireland
1597	Jonson *The Case is Altered* Shakespeare *The Merchant of Venice*	Private Blackfriars Theatre constructed
1599	Shakespeare *Julius Caesar*	Satires proscribed and burnt. Globe Theatre opens
1600	Marston *Antonio's Revenge* Shakespeare *Hamlet*	Fortune Theatre opens. East India Company founded. Children of the Chapel at the Blackfriars Theatre
1601	Dekker *Satiromastix* Jonson *Poetaster* Shakespeare *Twelfth Night*	Essex's rebellion and execution. Defeat of joint Irish/Spanish army in Ireland
1603	Jonson *Sejanus* Marston *The Malcontent*	Death of Elizabeth; accession of James I. Lord Chamberlain's Men become the King's Men
1604	Chapman *Bussy D'Ambois* Shakespeare *Measure for Measure* Shakespeare *Othello*	
1605	Middleton *A Mad World, My Masters* Shakespeare *King Lear*	Gunpowder Plot

	Plays and playwrights	Theatre and politics
1606	Jonson *Volpone* Middleton *Michaelmas Term* Middleton *The Revenger's Tragedy* Shakespeare *Macbeth*	
1607	Shakespeare *Antony and Cleopatra*	
1608		King's Men lease the Blackfriars Theatre
1610	Beaumont and Fletcher *The Maid's Tragedy* Jonson *The Alchemist*	
1611	Dekker and Middleton *The Roaring Girl* Jonson *Catiline* Shakespeare *The Winter's Tale* Shakespeare *The Tempest*	Authorised Version of the Bible published
1612	Webster *The White Devil*	
1613		Overbury scandal begins. Globe Theatre burns down
1614	Jonson *Bartholomew Fair* Webster *The Duchess of Malfi*	
1615	Middleton and Rowley *A Fair Quarrel*	
1616	Jonson *The Devil is an Ass* Middleton *The Witch* Shakespeare dies	Jonson Folio published
1617	Webster *The Devil's Lawcase*	Jonson made Poet Laureate
1618		Thirty Years War begins

	Plays and playwrights	Theatre and politics
1621	Middleton *Women Beware Women*	
1622	Middleton and Rowley *The Changeling*	
1623		Prince Charles's unsuccesful visit to Spain to marry the Infanta. Shakespeare First Folio published
1624	Middleton *A Game at Chess*	
1625		James I dies; accession of Charles I
1626	Jonson *The Staple of News*	
1627	Middleton dies	Failure of La Rochelle expedition
1628		Petition of Right
1629		Buckingham assassinated. Beginning of Charles I's personal rule
1630?	Ford *'Tis Pity She's a Whore*	
1632	Webster dies (?) Jonson *The Magnetic Lady*	
1637	Jonson dies	

Prologue: Webster's Aesthetic Relativism

John Webster was born into a world of rapid change. Old structures of society, of religion, and of trade were breaking down, to be replaced by a world which we would recognise as 'modern'. The centuries-long political and theological dominance of the Catholic church was being challenged across Europe by a number of new understandings of Christianity, grouped together under the term 'Protestantism'; cities were becoming larger, drawing in more people from the countryside and changing the nature of local communities; and in those cities, the beginnings of a world-wide trade economy were making themselves felt. In such an atmosphere of change, different people reacted in different ways. Some adopted a fixed religious position, going to their death for their beliefs: this occurred among both Catholics and Protestants. Some probably doubted the validity of religion entirely, but the power of the church was not yet weakened enough that such an opinion could be publicly uttered without fear of reprimand. Some embraced the new economy as a means of getting rich quick, trampling over whomever and whatever stood in their way; others complained of the unfairness and immorality of the economic system. Some strove to maintain what they saw as the ancient dignity of the English social system, with its concentration of power in the figure of the monarch; others mounted a radical challenge to that system, at one point in the seventeenth century eradicating monarchy from England, Scotland, Wales, and Ireland completely.

And then there were others, who seem to have adopted a position known as *relativism*: for relativists, there is no absolute truth, morality, or knowledge. All of these things exist only as part of a particular cultural system. To take an example, the violent debate between differing branches of Christianity in the Renaissance was, to those involved, literally a matter about *truth*. A relativist, however, would argue that the differing interpretations of Christianity do not refer to anything outside themselves; that is, that there is no truth *outside* the particular world-system which humans have created for themselves (which in this case, happens to involve a religion called Christianity). One can be a complete relativist, arguing that all standards of knowledge are constructed by humans. Alternatively, one can be more selective in one's relativism, arguing, for example, that morality is relative: that is, that no course of action (say, killing a human being) is *always and absolutely* right or wrong, but that different societies determine the morality of the act for themselves (so some societies may prohibit all killing of humans, some may allow killing in times of war, some may allow judicial execution, some may allow sacrifice to the gods, and so on).

It is impossible, of course, to infer a writer's beliefs and values on the basis of dramatic literature: the literary genre most attuned to conflict and debate, drama, demands the expression of opposing points of view. We cannot say for certain whether Webster was a moral relativist, a religious relativist, or so on, although such concepts are useful for thinking about characters in his plays. What this book will suggest, however, is that Webster was an *aesthetic relativist*: that is, that his conception of drama did not privilege any forms, techniques, or genres (for example, tragedy or soliloquy) as *intrinsically* better than others. Webster's importance as a dramatist, this book will argue, is in this radical challenge to the aesthetic orthodoxies of his day; considering Webster as an aesthetic relativist also helps to explain why eras which prized the concept of absolute truth (the nineteenth century, for example) found Webster puzzling, and why our own era, in which relativism is as fashionable as it has ever been, has so enthusiastically adopted Webster as a major literary figure.

It should be stated that many, perhaps most, Webster scholars may not agree with my characterisation of Webster as an aesthetic relativist. To my knowledge, no one has yet suggested this as the determining principle behind Webster's dramatic output. The reader should be careful, then, of assuming that what I write is uncontested or uncontestable; but a reader in tune with the spirit of Webster should, of course, have no problem with accepting such uncertainty.

CHAPTER I

A London Life

LIFE

Despite his reputation as an enigmatic figure, John Webster had an early life which was as conventional as those of his main characters is spectacular. His life appears to have been lived entirely in and around the metropolis of London. London was, of course, the largest city in early modern England, and central to the cultural and commercial life of the country. The dramatist's father, also called John Webster, was born in London in 1550, and set himself up in business as a coach and wagon maker. The family business, and hence the family home, was located in Cow Lane, on the edge of Smithfield Market in Northwest London (just outside the city walls). A major growth industry in the sixteenth and seventeenth centuries, the wagon business sustained John Webster senior in relative comfort; after his death, the business was taken over by his youngest son Edward (although John junior may have contributed to the business in some manner). As a new industry in early modern London, the wagon makers had no guild of their own (the 'guilds' were associations of craftsmen and merchants, who often wielded considerable power within the city). They were, however, allowed to join the guild of the Merchant Taylors, and John Webster senior became a significant figure within the organisation.

In 1577 Webster's father married Elizabeth Coates, and John

junior was born soon after, probably between 1578 and 1580. Edward was born some considerable time later (c.1590–1), and it seems likely that there were also daughters in the family (many of the parish records were destroyed in the Great Fire of 1666, and it is difficult to speak with certainty about many aspects of Webster's family life). As his father was a prominent member of the Merchant Taylors' Guild, it seems likely that John Webster would have attended the Merchant Taylors' School, among the most esteemed schools in sixteenth-century London. The guiding force behind the school was the famed educationalist Richard Mulcaster, author of the influential treatises *Positions* (1581) and *The First Part of the Elementarie* (1582). Among other innovations, Mulcaster was a keen supporter of the use of drama as a pedagogical tool, and it may well have been at the Merchant Taylors' School that Webster received his first introduction to playing.

Webster probably entered school around 1587–9, and in 1598 he was admitted to the Middle Temple, one of the Inns of Court. The Inns of Court – Gray's Inn, the Middle Temple, the Inner Temple, and Lincoln's Inn – although primarily intended to train young men to practice as lawyers (then, as now, a prestigious and financially sound career choice) were popularly known as 'the third university' (the first two, of course, were the medieval institutions of Oxford and Cambridge). We do not know what drove Webster to study at the Inns of Court: he may have intended to become a lawyer, changing his mind at a later date and entering the theatre (as seems to have been the case with a contemporary playwright, John Marston), or he may have seen a legal training as a useful resource for contributing to the family business. Certainly attending the Inns of Court allowed him to remain in London, close to both the business and the theatre, and appears to have provided him with a legal training which he would later put to significant dramatic use in the trial scenes which are at the heart of many of his plays.

In 1606, when he was aged between 26 and 28, Webster married Sara Peniall. The marriage was conducted in some haste (requiring a special dispensation to be performed in Lent) and it seems clear that this was due to Sara being in the advanced stages of pregnancy: two months after the wedding, she gave birth to a son, also christened John. Contemporary documents indicate that the Websters had more children but, again, the loss of the parish records has ensured that we don't know how many, or when they were born. At the time of his marriage, Webster was already working in the professional theatre, although he was engaged solely in the practice of collaboration, composing plays as a member of a writing team. It was not until the next decade of the century that he would develop his reputation through the composition of sole-authored plays.

In 1615, however, around the time that Webster *was* developing a significant reputation as a dramatist of considerable skill, he claimed membership of the Merchant Taylors' Guild, the professional organisation to which his father had of course belonged. The reasons for making this choice at this time are not entirely clear: the decision may well have been related to the death of his father, particularly if, as recent biographers increasingly believe to be the case, Webster remained engaged in some capacity with the wagon business even throughout the years of his dramatic career.

After this date, there is little surviving documentary evidence relating to Webster apart, of course, from the literary and dramatic material (discussed below). Although the date of his death is estimated at some time in the 1630s, in reality the exact date and location of his birth, and the location of his burial, remain unknown.

EARLY MODERN LONDON

As a member of the commercial classes in early modern London, Webster was born into a city undergoing profound change. London had long been the largest city in England, but throughout the sixteenth and seventeenth centuries its dominance became even more pronounced. Economic developments at this time contributed to real and noticeable changes in society. For example, a new type of economy, anticipating in many ways the later capitalist economies of Western Europe and North America, was beginning to emerge in London and other major trading centres in the late sixteenth century, and individuals and groups engaged in trade, manufacturing and the professions – including the legal professions – became increasingly significant in social terms, and began to exercise considerable cultural influence.

This growth in financial capital was matched by a rapid acceleration in the rate of population increase in the late sixteenth and early seventeenth century. The figures speak for themselves: in 1550 London's population was 75,000; in 1600 it was 200,000; while in 1650 it was 400,000. This made it easily the largest settlement in England. Just as importantly, the growth of London was not matched by the growth of its commercial rivals on the continent. In 1550 five Western European cities had larger populations than London (Naples, Venice, Paris, Lisbon, and Antwerp), by 1600 that number had been reduced to just two (Naples and Paris), while in 1650 only Paris had a larger population than London. The dates of Webster's dramatic career, then, correspond to a huge increase in the number of people resident in London (and hence, of course, to an increase in potential audience numbers), but also to the growth of London as a European economic power.

Such an increase in population was due in part to extensive immigration, both from other parts of England and from the continent. This immigration was fuelled largely by the economic explosion that took place in early modern London, establishing the city as a major centre for international trade. As Ian Archer has pointed out, in the middle of the sixteenth century, London's mercantile economy was dominated by the cloth trade, and as such was heavily reliant on the fortunes of Antwerp, the continental centre of that trade. By the later sixteenth century, however, the expansion of London-based merchants into trade networks in the Baltic, the Mediterranean, and even the East Indies had changed the economic situation profoundly. From a city dominated by the cloth trade, London became an import-led economy, a market for the most exclusive of luxury commodities. This had, of course, a significant effect on the professional and social life of the city. The increase in imports led to an expansion in certain manufacturing industries (shipbuilding, silk weaving), and the number, size, and variety of shops in the city also increased hugely (Archer 1991). The nature of economics was beginning to change too: lending money at interest had traditionally been viewed as a sinful activity, condemned by biblical authority. But a developing credit market was clearly in existence in London at the beginning of the seventeenth century, even if it was still in its early stages. So the change in economic circumstances affected not just how people made their living: it also affected how they lived their lives, their expectations and aspirations, and even their conception of morality.

What is true of economics is also true of social hierarchy: early modern London had a society which, for the time, was remarkably mobile, calling into question traditional class boundaries. Not everyone was happy with this, of course, but as the period drew on, the distinction between inherited wealth ('the gentry') and acquired wealth (the commercial classes, merchants, or 'citizens') became less clear-cut, as growing intermarriage between the 'old' and 'new' families of wealth became increasingly common in the early seventeenth century. As Chapter 2 makes clear, such social tensions were frequently staged in the popular drama of the period.

If the economic climate and the social hierarchy of early modern London was in transition, so too was the religious – and hence political – atmosphere of the city, the country, and the continent. Reformation, of course, swept across Europe in the sixteenth century, as national churches variously elected to stay within the Roman Catholic church, or to become a Reformed (Protestant) institution. By Webster's time, the religious culture of the Church of England had become effectively Protestant, having been 'officially' Protestant since 1558, with Protestantism probably being accepted by most English people by the 1580s. The decades spanning the end of the sixteenth and the beginning of the seventeenth centuries witnessed the development of a self-consciously 'English' form of Protestantism, the much-lauded 'middle way' between conservative Catholicism and radical 'Puritanism'. But if a coherent religious identity was coalescing at the point at which Webster was writing, it was doing so in the wake of a century of religious indeterminacy and (often violent) upheaval. The unsettled nature of sixteenth-century English Christianity continued to have an impact on the seventeenth-century cultural life of the country, eventually contributing significantly to the chaos of the civil wars which broke out in the 1640s.

At the beginning of the sixteenth century, by contrast, England was, to all intents and purposes, secure and settled as a member of the universal (Roman Catholic) church. The break with the church, when it came in the 1530s, was not primarily the result of popular dissatisfaction or anger with clerical corruption, as earlier historiography has often claimed, but was instead directly related to Henry VIII's dynastic politics, in particular his desire for a divorce from his first wife, Catherine of Aragon, in order to marry his mistress, Anne Boleyn. Henry's theological rationale, which he may well have believed at some level, was that, as Catherine was the widow of Henry's elder brother, Henry's marriage was thus against God's will, and hence destined to fail to produce a male heir. Both theologically and politically, this argument was unacceptable to Rome, and the initial break between the churches followed this impasse. Although this eventually allowed the development of what would become English Protestantism ('Anglicanism'), it is difficult to accurately apply the term 'Protestant' to Henry, whose theological convictions wavered, often in line with political crises. As a result, those radical Protestants in 1530s England, who were few but vocal, could feel rather dissatisfied with the position of the church under the monarch.

Henry's death in 1547 led to the accession of his young son Edward VI, who in conjunction with his senior advisors set out to make England more 'fully' Protestant. Edward's reign, however, was brief, and when he died in 1553 he was succeeded by his half-sister Mary, Henry's daughter by his first wife, and a devout Catholic. Mary immediately set about reinstalling Catholicism as the state religion of England, and with her Spanish connections (both her mother and husband were Spanish) and papal support, England became a Catholic nation once again. Mary, though, also ruled briefly, and after her death in 1558 she was succeeded by Henry's daughter by Anne Boleyn, Elizabeth. Elizabeth immediately brought about the move to a moderate form of Protestantism which was to shape the English church for almost the next century.

The differences between Catholicism and Protestantism (in its various forms) are many, but two are especially important for understanding what is distinctive about English Protestantism. The first is the question of church governance. Whereas Catholics believed that the Pope was the representative of God on earth, and that the hierarchical structure of the church was divinely ordained, most Protestants preached what has become known as the doctrine of the priesthood of all believers: that is, that a member of the faithful did not need a priest, let alone a bishop or cardinal, to gain access to God. All Protestants rejected the spiritual authority of the Pope, viewing his power as entirely worldly, and most questioned the structure of church hierarchy. Some Protestants, known as Presbyterians, thought that bishops should also be abolished, and that church authority should be determined from below, collectively, rather than imposed from above. The other important question is sacramental theology. The chief rituals of the church were known as the sacraments, and the most important of these was the sacrament of the eucharist. Catholics believed that in the sacrament of the eucharist, the bread and wine were really changed into the body and blood of Christ. Protestants rejected this idea, but disagreed amongst themselves as to what happened in the eucharist: some thought that Christ was 'spiritually' present in the sacrament, others that the ritual was simply a way of remembering and commemorating Christ's death. English Protestantism adopted a stance on these two issues which was distinctive from most other churches: rejecting the doctrine of the real presence in the eucharist, English Protestantism nevertheless maintained a system of church governance (known as Episcopalianism) which maintained bishops and archbishops, but rejected cardinals and the Pope. In structure, then, the English church remained similar to what it had been before the Reformation (albeit shorn of continental links), but in theological terms it was quite different. It has been argued that most of Elizabeth's subjects at the time of her accession probably held Catholic sympathies, while her ruling classes were largely Protestant (Duffy 1992). This may be one way of explaining the curiously hybrid nature of the English church.

Protestantism, then, took some time to become the religion of the majority in England, but Elizabeth's long reign certainly helped English Protestantism to establish itself. Catholicism did not disappear completely, although as older generations died out, the old religion became less common. After Elizabeth's excommunication by the Pope in 1570, Jesuits were dispatched to England as missionaries, but in some ways this added to a popular anti-Catholicism developing in the late-sixteenth century; so too did the remarkable defeat of the Spanish Armada in 1588, a victory which convinced many English Protestants that God really was on their side. By the late sixteenth and early-seventeenth century, then, Catholicism was arguably less of a threat to the established Church of England than were those radical Protestants, often dismissively referred to as 'Puritans', who wished the church to become more emphatically 'Reformed', removing many of the liturgical features which such men saw as remnants of Catholicism. Webster's Italian Catholics of the seventeenth century, then, are 'imaginative' Catholics: Webster himself would have had no memory of English Catholicism, as the southeast of the country had been one of the earliest regions to adopt Protestantism with considerable enthusiasm; this should be borne in mind when considering the religious and political significance of Webster's plays.

The monarch under whom Webster composed most of his work was not Elizabeth, who died in 1603, but her successor, James VI of Scotland and I of England, the first Stuart king of England (Elizabeth, of course, was the last of the Tudors). James was a Protestant, but his mother had been a committed Catholic, and he saw himself as a peacemaker and a diplomat; to that end, he pursued as far as possible a policy of pacifism and non-confrontation, in religious as in political matters. He even went so far as to consider a Spanish marriage for his son, an episode which demonstrated a certain lack of understanding as to the – by that stage firmly Protestant – sympathies of most of his subjects. But the internal religious disputes of James's reign were primarily between differing factions of Protestantism, and the Italian Catholics found in Webster's tragedies were encountered most often on the stage for ordinary Londoners.

The relationship between economics, politics, and religion was always of some significance, of course, to a practising playwright like Webster. Although theatre was regarded by most practitioners and audiences as primarily a form of entertainment – the play texts of the period were not considered high literature in the way that drama can be now – nevertheless the theatre frequently engaged with political and religious issues. Often, of course, such issues were addressed indirectly, or glanced at from aside; this was necessary in an age when treason, for example, was punishable by death (and what counted as treason could change from time to time; under Elizabeth, for example, any Catholic supporting the supremacy of the Pope within the realm of England was answerable to the political charge of treason, rather then the religious charge of heresy). Occasionally, however, especially during the reign of James, dramatists and players showed themselves more willing to tackle controversial public issues. Playwrights could claim to be serving a legitimate social function in this way, as classical theories of tragedy in particular emphasised the advisory function of the artist. The Elizabethan poet and courtier Sir Philip Sidney, for example, displayed such classical influence when he argued that tragedy 'maketh kings fear to be tyrants, and tyrants manifest their tyrannical humours' (Sidney 2006: 965). But theory is one thing, practice often another; nowhere is this clearer than in the case of the dramatist Ben Jonson, imprisoned for writing dramatic satires both in the reign of Elizabeth (for *The Isle of Dogs*, 1597, with Thomas Nashe) and of James (for *Eastward Ho*, 1605, with George Chapman and John Marston; a response of sorts to Webster and Dekker's *Westward Ho*, 1604). Similarly, Thomas Middleton's 1625 satire *A Game at Chess*, which was a response to James's plan for a 'Spanish Match' (see p. 11), was a huge commercial success, enjoying an unprecedented run of nine days before being suppressed (playing companies normally played a different play every day to cater for a demanding audience; Middleton's play was therefore extraordinarily popular). So the theatre could relate to the wider religious and political discourses of early modern London in a variety of ways. It also, of course, played a significant role in the changing economy of the city. While the theatre was indeed an arena for political debate, it was also – and probably more importantly for those who made their living by the trade – a place where money could be made and careers built. The surviving 'diary' of the theatre entrepreneur, Philip Henslowe, for example, is actually an account book, detailing his expenditure, his debts and loans, and his payments (Henslowe 2002). If trade was changing the face of early modern London, this change was apparent also in the professional theatre, which had been a commercial enterprise from the moment of its inception.

Nowhere, perhaps, is the influence of the city more apparent in Webster's work than in *Monuments of Honour*, the triumph he wrote for the Lord Mayor's Pageant in 1624. Lord Mayor's Day took place on 29 October each year, 'a day of pageantry and ceremonial [. . .] on the occasion of the new Lord Mayor of London taking his oath of allegiance to the king' (Webster 2007: 223). The fact that the Lord Mayor this year, Sir John Gore, was a member of the Merchant Taylors' Guild may well explain why Webster was chosen to compose the pageant, the only time he was asked to do so. Certainly the dramatist made the most of the spectacular opportunities afforded by the pageant form, ensuring that this 'particularly ambitious example of the triumph genre' was not only one of the most spectacular, but also 'one of the most expensive ever' (Webster 2007: 224).

Two institutions and one individual come in for special praise in Webster's triumph. The individual is Prince Henry, son of the reigning King James VI and I; Henry had died eight years previously, and had been himself allied to the Merchant Taylors (his death seems to have had a lasting effect on Webster, who also composed the poem *A Monumental Column* in praise of the prince). The two institutions which are praised, fitting for both the thrust of the particular pageant and Webster's own personal interests, are the Merchant Taylors' Guild and the City of London; the city and guild are consistently linked together and presented as, in the words of one critic, 'pre-eminent exemplars of honour' (Webster 2007: 233).

The praise of London is particularly interesting in the light of the social and economic changes to the city discussed above. Webster presents London as a major capital in the new European order, a revival of the great cities of the classical world, and a magnet for the rest of the world. In the triumph's opening pageant, two actors representing the allegorical figures of Thetis and Oceanus discuss the great city which is apparent to their sight. Thetis begins by confusing the city for one of the most renowned of all maritime locations: 'Sure this is Venice'. He is corrected, however, by the more knowledgeable Oceanus: 'That beauteous seate is *London* so much fam'd, / Where any Nauigable Sea is nam'd' (Webster 2007: 251). London, it is claimed, has become famous throughout the world, so much so that the Oceans themselves come to pay tribute.

The Oceanus episode takes place on the water, in the Thames itself. When the spectacle moves onto the land, and hence into the city proper, London's pre-eminence is again displayed, this time in a pageant described by Webster as follows:

> In the highest seate a Person representing *Troynouant* ['New-Troy'] or the City, inthroned in rich Habilaments, beneath her as admiring her peace and felicity, sit fiue eminent cities, as *Antwerpe*, *Paris*, *Rome*, *Venice* and *Constantinople*. (Webster 2007: 252)

Again this can be usefully compared to the growth of London, both economically and demographically, in the period. Not only is London a truly 'Renaissance' city (it is the 'New Troy', a common conceit among pro-civic writers of the period), it also towers over the major cities of Europe and the Ottoman Empire. If proof were needed that Webster was aware of the European and global influence increasingly wielded by London, *Monuments of Honour*, even acknowledging its ceremonial elaborations, certainly provides it.

DRAMATIC AND LITERARY CAREER

The earliest evidence of Webster's writing for the stage comes in the 'diary' of Philip Henslowe. In the entry for 22 May 1602, Henslowe notes a payment to the collaborative team of Michael Drayton, Thomas Middleton, Anthony Munday, and Webster for a play called *Caesar's Fall*. A week later, another entry lists another payment to the same team (with an extra member, Thomas Dekker), for the completion of a play called *Two Shapes*; most critics believe that *Two Shapes* and *Caesar's Fall* are alternate names for the same play, which has since been lost. Although the play no longer survives, nevertheless this evidence allows us to see how Webster worked at this point of his career; that is, as a participant in the very common Renaissance practice of collaborative authorship. Typically in a collaborative endeavour, the structure of the play would be sketched out by the dramatists, and each member of the team would be responsible for writing particular scenes. Such a method of composition, very different to that of modern playwrights, helped to ensure that there was a constant turnover of new plays to feed the demands of the early modern audience. It may also have introduced Webster to a variety of genres, techniques, and approaches to composition which would influence his later aesthetic relativism. Later in 1602, Webster was part of another large playwrighting team (along with Henry Chettle, Dekker, Thomas Heywood, and one Mr. Smythe), who received payment for a two-part play known as *Lady Jane* (this survives in a one-part printed version known as *Sir Thomas Wyatt*; the exact relationship between *Lady Jane* and *Sir Thomas Wyatt* is unclear). Also that year, he collaborated with Chettle, Dekker, and Heywood on *Christmas Comes But Once a Year*, which has also been lost.

It has been speculated that these plays represent a kind of 'apprenticeship' for Webster, a way of learning the craft of playwriting in the company of more senior professionals (Gunby 2004). His next dramatic undertakings seem to have been at a slightly more senior level. In 1604, Webster's name appears, along with that of John Marston, on the title-page of *The Malcontent*, a play which the latter had written for performance by the Children of the Chapel (or Blackfriars Boys), one of the child playing troupes popular in early modern London. There were two major boy troupes: the Children of the Chapel, whose members were recruited from the choristers of the Chapel Royal, and who acted in the Blackfriars theatre, and the Children of Paul's (or Paul's Boys), whose members were drawn from the choristers of St. Paul's Cathedral, and who played in a specially-adapted part of the Cathedral. The boys' companies were commercial rivals both with each other, and with the adult companies. Webster's additions to the play – an Induction and several comic scenes – resulted from the 'appropriation' of the play by the leading adult company of the day, the King's Men. Part of Webster's task, then, was to explain the rather delicate matter of the 'theft' of the play by the King's Men; it is generally agreed that Webster's additions are very skilfully handled. Also in 1604, Webster collaborated with Dekker on *Westward Ho*, a city comedy written for performance by the Children of Paul's. Following Jonson, Chapman, and Marston's 'sequel', *Eastward Ho*, Webster and Dekker responded with a 'sequel' of their own, *Northward Ho*, performed in 1605.

Both the *Ho* plays and *Sir Thomas Wyatt* were published in 1607, and it would be some time before Webster would return to the stage. When he did, though, it was with *The White Devil*, first performed in 1612 by Queen Anne's Men, at the Red Bull in Clerkenwell. Although now regarded as among the finest of Webster's achievements, the play failed to find an appreciative audience at the Red Bull, an outdoor theatre primarily known for staging rather unsophisticated, militaristic 'drum-and-trumpet' plays, a genre worlds away from Webster's sophisticated tragedy (Gurr 2004). Perhaps as a result of the poor reception, and perhaps as an attempt to demonstrate its poetic strengths, Webster oversaw the publication of the play in the same year, a remarkably rapid publication for a Renaissance play-text. Also in 1612, Webster composed the most significant of his non-dramatic verse, *A Monumental Column*, a long elegy commemorating the death of Henry, Prince of Wales, eldest son of James VI of Scotland and I of England. Strong verbal links between *A Monumental Column* and *The Duchess of Malfi* suggest that Webster was already at work on his second major tragedy at this point.

The Duchess was performed by the King's Men in 1614, at the prestigious indoors Blackfriars theatre, where the reception was much warmer than that afforded *The White Devil* at the Red Bull; the play stayed in the company's repertoire for some time, and also enjoyed outdoor performance at the rebuilt Globe (the first having burned down in 1613). Now generally regarded as Webster's masterpiece, and as the play which most clearly crystallises his distinctive worldview, the play was an immediate success. It may have been followed by a third major tragedy: documents from the period, including some composed by Webster himself, refer to a play known only as *Guise*, apparently written by Webster as sole author, and presumably based on the life of the French nobleman the Duke of Guise. This play has been lost, and – if the assumption that this was indeed a third sole-authored tragedy is correct – this is perhaps the most significant (and hence most disappointing) non-survival of all the plays in which Webster had a hand.

In 1615, Webster interrupted his dramatic career to contribute a series of thirty-two prose 'characters' (brief personality sketches of character types or occupations) to the sixth edition of Sir Thomas Overbury's *The Wife*, a hugely popular book in Jacobean London. By 1618 he was writing for the stage again, producing his last sole-authored play, the tragicomedy *The Devil's Law-Case*, for performance by the Queen's Men at the new indoor Cockpit in Drury Lane. Although the play has traditionally been overlooked in favour of the two tragedies, recent scholarship has begun to re-evaluate, and to stress the accomplishment of, this play.

After *The Devil's Law-Case*, it seems that Webster never wrote another play unaided, although he did continue to collaborate with other dramatists for another decade or so. In 1621 he wrote the city comedy *Anything for a Quiet Life*, with Thomas Middleton, and, in 1624, *A Cure for a Cuckold* with Heywood and Rowley (considered by many readers to be the most successful of all Webster's collaborative pieces). Also in 1624 he undertook the composition of *Monuments of Honour*, his only Lord Mayor's Pageant (see pp. 12–14). In 1625, he collaborated with John Ford and Philip Massinger on a play left unfinished by the death of John Fletcher, *The Fair Maid of the Inn*, and in 1626 or 1627 he completed his last work for the stage, the classically-inspired tragedy *Appius and Virginia*, written with Thomas Heywood.

Webster's dramatic output is not overly copious for a professional dramatist of the English Renaissance; indeed, many contemporaries explicitly criticised him for his perceived slowness of composition. However, many of the plays in which he was involved were extremely popular in their day, and remain well-regarded now: the *Ho* plays, *The Devil's Law-Case*, and *A Cure for a Cuckold*, for example. And the two plays on which his reputation as a major dramatist rest, *The White Devil* and *The Duchess of Malfi*, while they have had their detractors (among the Victorians, especially), are now generally regarded as among the greatest plays of the English Renaissance.

CHAPTER 2

Textual Culture: Webster's Collaborative Drama

RENAISSANCE DRAMA AND THE PRACTICE OF COLLABORATION

Although John Webster is now regarded as one of the most distinctive voices of the English Renaissance – a reputation which derives largely from *The White Devil* and *The Duchess of Malfi*, which are taken to represent a distinctively 'Websterian' vision – nevertheless, the vast majority of his dramatic output was written in collaboration with one or (often) more other dramatists. In this, Webster was not alone: most professional dramatists in the period composed in collaboration at one point or other of their careers, and some critics claim that collaborative, rather than individual, composition was the 'norm' for the industry (Masten 1997: 4). How did such collaboration work in practical terms? The answer seems to be far from straightforward; as far as can be ascertained, indeed, there is no one answer. Different texts were composed in different ways, according to the styles and expertise of the dramatists involved, and the type of work being undertaken (evidence survives, for example, of dramatists being employed to make additions or revisions to earlier plays, as well as to compose wholly new ones). The most common way for collaborative writers to work in the period was probably to use the play's outline to divide up acts and scenes between themselves, and then for each writer initially to compose their parts more or less in isolation from their colleagues (Ioppolo 2006: 32). Critical history has tended to overlook collaborative pieces at the expense of sole-authored ones, although this may result in an inaccurate view of what was clearly a very important professional activity.

Reinstalling collaboration as an important paradigm for Renaissance dramatic composition raises many taxing questions both about how writers worked in the Renaissance, and about how modern readers engage with that work. Many critics, for example, are now very suspicious about using the term 'the author' to refer to the composer of a Renaissance text (even one which appears to have been composed solely by one dramatist), as the modern concept of 'the author' is held to apply only to a view of the world which crystallises in the period known as the European Enlightenment. According to this viewpoint, all the things which the concept of 'the author' suggests – a unitary coherence, a single viewpoint, a clear relation between the producer of the text and the form and content of the text itself – are anachronistic when applied to early modern England. This viewpoint also accords with the way in which 'the author' has been imagined in literary theory of the second half of the twentieth century. Two extremely influential theorists – Roland Barthes and Michel Foucault – argue that the mystique and authority located in the concept of 'an author' is misguided, and that all texts – literary, dramatic, or otherwise – are social constructs, composed and understood according to social rules and assertions, rather than being the output of a single, inspired consciousness (Barthes 1977; Foucault 2003).

Such an approach to thinking about authorship brings serious benefits, but also some potential disadvantages, both when thinking about Renaissance drama in general, and the case of Webster in particular. On the positive side, challenging the 'authority' of 'the author' allows critics and readers to re-evaluate the significance of those collaborative pieces long overlooked by audiences; in the case of Webster, of course, this means that many of the plays which have not been frequently read or studied can be engaged with in a way which does not explicitly compare them to *The White Devil*, *The Duchess of Malfi*, and *The Devil's Law-Case*. This allows us to think of these plays in a different way, to consider them as documents of a fascinating moment in Western cultural history. On the other hand, of course, most critics and audiences have found the greatest value in precisely those texts of Webster's which are his work alone, and the links between these plays – in terms of their shared imagery, their cultural and dramatic preoccupations – may suggest to some readers that there is a continued relevance in using the term 'Websterian' to refer to the common features which *The White Devil*, *The Duchess of Malfi*, and, to some extent, *The Devil's Law-Case* share, and hence in supporting the idea of John Webster as an 'author' of some significance.

Where, then, does this leave the collaborative drama, which was extremely popular in its day? Another factor to consider might be the relationship between performance and print, both in the Renaissance and now. The two plays taken to be most characteristic of Webster's concerns, *The White Devil* and *The Duchess of Malfi*, are easily available in a variety of modern editions. This, of course, is convenient for modern bookshops, which have an investment in the idea of the author. Collaborative drama is much more difficult to fit into a modern conception of 'the book', which as a commodity is chiefly identifiable by the twin category of author and title. The early modern conception of the printed book, however, is rather different, as many printed editions of playbooks did not even print the name of the author on the title page (the name of the acting company is much more common, lending weight to the idea that the early modern theatre was primarily a collaborative industry). But even this is not straightforward, for the early editions of *The White Devil* and *The Duchess of Malfi* contain examples of a mode of thought developing in the period, of a distinction between the play as performed (to be seen/heard) and the play as printed (to be read). The latter, scholars like Lukas Erne have argued, is a more self-consciously 'literary' text (often longer, often more sophisti-cated in terms of character development and motivation) which indeed might gesture towards a modern conception of 'the author' (Erne 2003: 27).

So there is not a consensus as to the cultural significance attached to 'individual', as opposed to 'collaborative' works in the Renaissance, although most current critics are more willing to engage with collaborative works than has been the case in the past. What follows in this chapter is an introduction to the collaborative works which Webster is known to have a hand in, and a guide to how they might fit into Webster's larger dramatic career, and into the posthumous process of criticism and appreciation of the dramatist. The chapter is divided into two sections: 'Early Collaborative Pieces' examines those plays thought to have been composed before Webster's three sole-authored pieces (four, of course, if the lost *Guise* is included in the number), and 'Late Collaborative Pieces' examines those plays thought to have been composed after *The White Devil*, *The Duchess of Malfi*, and *The Devil's Law-Case*.

EARLY COLLABORATIVE PIECES

Caesar's Fall, or, Two Shapes (1602) and *Christmas Comes But Once a Year* (1602) have both been lost, so there is relatively little that can be said about Webster's earliest dramatic writings; critics have speculated that these were aimed at a popular market (Gunby 2004), which seems likely, although there is clearly no direct evidence as to the form of the plays. Our knowledge of the existence of these plays, however, does alert us to the fact that Webster's first professional engagement with the world of the Renaissance theatre was as a collaborative dramatist, a fact which may alert us to the potential significance of this for his later career.

The first play of Webster's which survives is *The Famous History of Sir Thomas Wyatt*, printed in 1607, but initially composed as *Lady Jane* in 1602, in collaboration with Chettle, Dekker, Heywood, and Smith. As the title suggests, this is a history play, although it is unlike Shakespeare's history plays both in the date of composition (which is considerably later than Shakespeare's Elizabethan history plays), and in the events depicted (which are much more recent than those depicted by Shakespeare). The play deals with the events surrounding the death of Edward VI and the accession of Mary I, and has a dual focus (as indicated by its alternate titles). One strand of the play focuses on the political intrigues behind the proclamation of Lady Jane Grey as Queen of England; Jane is presented as unambitious and unassuming, an unwilling victim of the power politics of noble men; her trial and execution form the finale of the play. The other strand focuses on the titular

Thomas Wyatt (not the Renaissance poet of the same name, but rather a Kentish landowner). Wyatt is faithful to the memory of Henry VIII, and this leads him to rebel on two occasions in the play: firstly, against the proclamation of Jane as opposed to Henry's daughter, Mary, and secondly, against Mary's plans to marry the Spanish Prince Philip. This second rebellion sees Wyatt lead a force against the city of London, as a result of which he is condemned for treason. As an English history play, *Sir Thomas Wyatt* is unique in Webster's oeuvre, although it is striking that the question of female rulers, and their relationship to the networks of masculine power which surround them, are significant preoccupations of this play, much as they would be of Webster's later works.

The Malcontent, a tragicomedy with an intensely satiric focus on courtly corruption, was composed by the playwright John Marston for performance by the Chapel Children in 1603. Two editions of the play, both printed in 1604, probably reflect the play as it was performed by its original playing company. However, the play was appropriated by the King's Men, the leading adult company, and it appears that Webster was hired to write additional passages for this adult production. The third edition of the play, also printed in 1604, contains Webster's additions. The purpose of the additions was threefold: to justify the unconventional appropriation of a rival company's playing text (Webster achieves this through a remarkable Induction, which insists that some of the King's Men's leading actors play themselves, in a moment of intense metatheatricality which well suits the play's overall emphasis on role-play and disguise); to extend the length of the play for adult performance; and to provide a substantial comic role for the King's Men's clown, Robert Armin. The latter two requirements are fulfilled by the invention of a new comic character, Passarello, although it is generally felt that the comic scenes are less successful than the Induction. Confusingly, Marston too seems to have written some of the extra passages included in the third edition (these may or may not have been cut from the first two editions), which adds to the considerable textual difficulties faced by editors of the play. The general editorial consensus is that the play as a whole should be credited to Marston, with the bulk of Webster's additions represented by the Induction and the extra comic scenes. The relationship between

Marston's and Webster's additions, however, remains unresolved. Keith Sturgess surmises that Marston's passages may have been part of his original plan for the play, which were cut for initial performances (and hence for initial publication); this would make Webster the sole 'reviser' of the play for performance by the King's Men (Marston 1997: xx). Charles Cathcart, however, has recently argued that both Marston and Webster may have composed their additions at the same time, each with some knowledge of what the other dramatist's plans were: this would mean that the two dramatists were, in a sense, collaborating on the revisions of the play (Cathcart 2006: 54). Whatever the case, we can be sure that Webster had a significant hand in *The Malcontent*'s transposition from the child company to the adult.

Webster's next two plays, both written in collaboration with Thomas Dekker, were popular examples of the city (or citizen) comedy genre, a genre which grew out of, and satirised, the emerging mercantile classes of early modern London. In *Westward Ho*, performed in 1604, young gallants try to seduce the wives of three London citizens, by persuading them to journey to the market town of Brentford, an area with a reputation in the early seventeenth century as a convenient spot for illicit sexual activity, particularly adultery (Morgan-Russell 1999: 70). The plot backfires on the gallants, however, as the three women, while agreeing to the journey, form a female community to outwit the men's erotic intentions. At the end of the play, the women return home to their husbands, fulfilling the social and generic conventions of comedy. In its emphasis on the parallels between the worlds of mercantile exchange and erotic encounter, and in its willingness to stage the criminal underworld of prostitution in early modern London, *Westward Ho* shares many of its concerns with other popular city comedies of the day.

Recent critical readings of the play have been interested in Dekker and Webster's portrayal of the city wives, particularly in so far as the women conceive of themselves as a coherent community. Simon Morgan-Russell, for example, has argued that the play suggests to its audience that 'male expectation of desire can be destroyed by the rebellion offered by an alliance of women' (Morgan-Russell 1999: 77). Michelle M. Dowd, meanwhile, suggests that the freedom afforded to the female characters in this play – not only are they the audience's main focus of attention, but they are able to roam around and beyond the city – offers 'male and female spectators alike an anxious caution about female economic control' (Dowd 2003: 227). Both critics agree that Webster and Dekker are staging some of the anxieties and concerns of their audience, an audience witnessing at first hand the social changes wrought by a changing economy.

Northward Ho (1604–5), the second of Webster and Dekker's *Ho* collaborations (but the third in the 'series', following *Eastward Ho* by Jonson, Chapman, and Marston), again follows the template of satirical city comedy. Thus the plot revolves around the sexual economy of the early modern city, the sexual availability (or otherwise) of the citizen wife (here Mistress Maybury) and the Prostitute (here, as often in the drama of the period, Dorothy or Doll). Two aspects of the play have attracted particular attention. The character Bellamont, identified as a poet and writer of dramatic sketches, exercised the biographical impulses of mid-twentieth-century critics, who attempted to prove that Bellamont was a satiric portrait of one or other English Renaissance dramatist (Schwartz 1959; Ornstein 1961; Gabel 1969). Such identifications were never concrete, and there is no indication in the play that Bellamont was intended by either Dekker or Webster to be read as an explicit portrait of another writer; neither is there any indication that early modern audiences reacted to the play in this way. Of more interest to recent critics has been the scene in which the citizens and gallants visit the hospital of 'Bedlam . . . Where the mad-men are.' 'Bedlam' is a corruption of 'Bethlehem', the shortened form of the Hospital of St Mary of Bethlehem, in Bishopsgate which, although founded as a priory, became a hospital for lunatics after the dissolution of the monasteries in the mid-sixteenth century. The play stages the spectacle of the 'mad-men' in a way that anticipates the dance of the madmen in Webster's later *Duchess of Malfi*, and which has been seen by critics as representative of the exploitation of social outcasts in early modern London. Ken Jackson, however, has argued that modern understandings of the representations of Bethlem (and its sister institution, Bridewell) in early modern drama can be overly simplistic, and that early modern audiences might well have associated the entertainment associated with spectacle of lunacy with a form of charity (Jackson 2003). Even this critic, however, is forced to admit that *Northward Ho* is less charitable than other plays: Bethlem here is 'a diversion in the play, used only to amuse' (Jackson 2003: 405).

LATE COLLABORATIVE PIECES

After *Northward Ho*, for some time Webster primarily worked alone in writing for the stage, producing *The White Devil*, *The Duchess of Malfi*, *Guise*, and *The Devil's Law-Case*. He returned to collaboration, and to the genre of city comedy, in 1621, writing *Anything for a Quiet Life* with the prolific dramatist Thomas Middleton. The play abounds in the kinds of trickery and disguise which were by this stage a common feature of the city comedy genre. The play's main focus is on the character of Cressingham, a widower who has remarried a woman much younger than himself. Ignoring the advice of his friends, Cressingham and his children seem throughout the course of the play to be at the mercy of the new Lady Cressingham, who even manages to sell the family's ancestral lands. It is only with an abrupt *volte-face* on the part of Lady Cressingham at the play's end that the harmony of the Cressingham family can be restored. A sub-plot focuses on the relationship between Walter Chamlet, a cloth merchant, and his wife Rachel. A third sub-plot focuses on the attempts of a Lord Beaufort to seduce the wife of Knaves-Bee, a lawyer. In its interest in the differing demands of domestic and public relationships, the play shares preoccupations with Webster's major tragedies, but it lacks the dizzying shifts in tone and perspective of those plays. The single exception is the dramatic reversal of the character of Lady Cressingham at the play's end, an abrupt example of Webster's characteristic juxtaposition of clashing dramatic tones.

Although Lady Cressingham is no Vittoria Corombona or Duchess of Malfi, she has, like her illustrious predecessors, tended to dominate critical discussion of the play. The central question with which critics have concerned themselves has been whether Lady Cressingham has been dissembling throughout (and thus was 'really' a virtuous character) or whether the end of the play stages a deeply unrealistic – and dramatically unsatisfactory – change in behaviour. There has been no critical consensus on this matter, and David Carnegie, in the most recent discussion of the question, acknowledges that 'Lady Cressingham is the most difficult character to analyze' (Webster 2007: 32), and suggests that 'it is possible that the playwrights have opted for what we might call an inconsistency convention, in which a naturalist coherence of psychology is eschewed in favour of an Early Modern emphasis on the motivation demanded by the plot in each scene' (Webster 2007: 33). This is more helpful than the suggestion that Lady Cressingham is *either* dissembling throughout *or* poorly written, but in some ways it does not go far enough. Webster's aesthetic relativism consists, in part, of a deliberate juxtaposition of different dramatic modes, and even of the presentation of the same character as possessing quite different characteristics in different scenes: Vittoria in *The White Devil* is perhaps the best example of this (see p. 74). Lady Cressingham is like Vittoria in that she is radically different at different parts of the play: there is no 'real' Lady Cressingham beneath the opposing portraits, which are left deliberately unresolved. This is a characteristically Websterian technique; the fact that it happens once, rather than on a number of occasions, does not make it any less so.

Webster's next play, *Keep the Widow Waking*, composed with Dekker, Ford, and Rowley in 1624, has not survived; *A Cure for a Cuckold*, written with Heywood and Rowley in 1624–5, has survived in a printed edition from 1661, and is another example of Webster writing a collaborative comedy. The plot of *A Cure for a Cuckold* combines 'aristocratic' romantic comedy with a more robust form of city comedy. In the main plot, Lessingham, a young gentleman, is in love with Clare, who rejects his advances, delivering to him a cryptic letter which Lessingham interprets as a challenge to kill his best friend in order to enjoy Clare's love. Meanwhile, Bonvile, another young gentleman, has just married Annabel, but before the marriage festivities can be completed (and the marriage consummated), Bonvile leaves to (as he thinks) second Lessingham in a duel. Lessingham's request, however, is a ploy to see which of his friends loves him best, and when the two young gentleman arrive in Calais (the supposed location of the duel), Lessingham reveals his plan to kill Bonvile. Bonvile escapes with his life by renouncing Lessingham's friendship forever, thereby ensuring that Lessingham has indeed 'killed' his best friend. When Lessingham returns to Clare, she is distraught at the news that Bonvile is dead; unknown to any of the characters on stage, Clare has been in love with Bonvile, and, frustrated at his marriage to Annabel, had intended the letter to serve as a coded instruction to Lessingham to kill Clare. Bonvile plots to bring Clare and Lessingham together, and the end of the aristocratic plot stages their marriage, reflecting that of Annabel and Bonvile at the play's opening. The 'citizen' plot, meanwhile, from which the play's title derives, dramatises the adventures of Compass, a sailor who, lost at sea and presumed dead, returns home to find that his wife has borne a son to another man in his absence. Compass, a naturally generous man, is happy to bring the son up as his own, but reluctant to live with the social stigma of being a cuckold. Hence he devises a plan to divorce Urse, his wife, and then to remarry her, thereby erasing the spectre of cuckoldry. At the play's close, the aristocratic and citizen worlds collide, and the marriage of Compass and Urse, like those of Annabel and Bonvile and Clare and Lessingham, stands as a symbol of a society returned to order.

Despite the fact that Webster's tragedies are far from consistent in their tone and technique, the similar lack of generic focus in his comedies has concerned many commentators. While *A Cure for a Cuckold* is clearly a comedy, the two plots are nevertheless very different in tone, and there has been some critical debate over the aesthetic effect of this disjunction. Of course, a reader who accepts the proposition that Webster was an aesthetic relativist will find this disjunction in tone, and indeed the broader move from tragedy to comedy, less difficult to comprehend. Jacqueline Pearson's idea that the play 'has a secure comic identity but undermines this by ironic contrasts' is useful, but she strives too hard to make the play fit into a conception of artistic success which stresses coherence and integrity: 'comedy and tragicomedy finally synthesize in images of marriage and music' (Pearson 1980: 132). On the contrary, Webster is an artist of discord, not of harmony: the move to comedy in the later stages of his career does not diminish this fact, despite the conventions of the comic form. Similar conceptions about the integrity of dramatic form have in part influenced critical discussions of Compass. For Pearson, although he appears in the 'subplot', he is nevertheless 'a central figure who provides a background of values more secure and sympathetic than those of the tragicomic plot' (Pearson 1980: 119). Again, there are certain assumptions about drama here which seem not to have been shared by Webster. The aesthetic relativism of Webster's drama means that it always shades towards a moral relativism, as well. While this might not mean that Webster was himself a moral relativist (early modern dramatic literature rarely offers insight into the beliefs of its author), it does mean that any attempt to determine the 'values' espoused by a Websterian play is bound to end in failure. In other words, it does not seem valid to claim that for the play, or the dramatist, the 'values' of Compass are any better (or, for that matter, any worse), than the 'values' of any of the aristocratic characters. There is, in fact, a clear early modern context for this kind of relativist thought about categories and values. For example, the French essayist Michel de Montaigne, whose *Essais* were translated into English in 1603, had a significant influence on English cultural thought: 'Not only each countrie, but every Cittie, yea and every vocation hath his owne particular decorum,' writes Montaigne (Montaigne 1603: 23), recalling the scepticism of the classical author Plutarch, who introduced his *Lives* with the proviso that (in Thomas North's early modern translation): 'beyonde this time all is full of suspicion and dout, being deliuered vs by Poets and Tragedy makers, sometimes without trueth and likelihoode, and alwayes with out certainty' (Plutarch 1579: 1). This may not necessarily negate René Weis' claim that Compass is 'one of the great comic characters of the Jacobean theatre' (Webster 1996: xxvi), but it does suggest that any 'greatness' which Compass possesses should not be interpreted as a moral one.

The next play in which Webster had a hand, *The Fair Maid of the Inn*, is a tragicomedy of the type fashionable in the 1620s. It seems to have begun life as a sole-authored play by the dramatist John Fletcher, the leading exponent of the genre; left uncompleted at Fletcher's death, it was reworked by a team including Webster and the playwrights John Ford and Philip Massinger. Like *A Cure for a Cuckold*, it dramatises two plots – one aristocratic, one plebeian – but is set in Italy rather than in England; and, in characteristically Fletcherian fashion, the apparently 'low-life' plot is actually nothing of the sort. The 'aristocratic' plot, like *The Duchess of Malfi*, centres on a brother-sister-suitor triangle. As in the earlier play, the brother (in this case called Caesario) attempts to prevent the marriage of the sister (here Clarissa) to a suitor (in this case Mentivole). Unlike the tragedy, the marriage in this play is neither clandestine nor doomed to fail, but instead forms part of a conventional comic resolution, blessed by Caesario. The 'plebeian' plot is focused on the inn of the title and on its 'fair maid', Bianca, who (it transpires) is 'really' an aristocrat, and is thus rewarded with marriage to Caesario. This is a play with Fletcher's imprint all over it and, whether out of his respect for his recently-deceased colleague, or whether because of his limited role in the composition of the play, Webster seems to have been unable to seriously subvert the conventional form of the drama (notwithstanding the fact that tragicomedy is the dramatic genre whose conventions most nearly approach the Websterian juxtaposition of tones and techniques).

The last play which Webster is thought to have composed, this time in collaboration with Thomas Heywood, is a return to the tragic genre with which he established his reputation. The classical tragedy *Appius and Virginia* opens with the promotion of Appius to a powerful position in the Roman senate, but with stirrings of discontent among the Roman soldiery. The spokesman for the soldiers' grievances, the noble commander Virginius, has travelled to Rome to address the senate; meanwhile his daughter, Virginia, is to be married to Icilius. Virginia is also, however, the object of the lust of Appius; the latter resolves to use his political position to thwart the demands of Virginius, thinking that this will aid him in his seduction of the soldier's daughter. Accordingly, Appius refuses Virginia's request for extra supplies for the soldiers. Virginius uses his time in the city to approve the marriage of his daughter to Icilius, and then rides back to the near-mutinous camp. In his absence, Marcus Clodius, Appius's servant, begins the task of wooing Virginia on Appius's behalf. Virginius returns to a camp on the verge of mutiny, the soldiers' rebellion checked only by their loyalty to their commander; to forestall mutiny, Virginius feels it necessary to lie to the soldiers about the reception of his case in the senate. In Rome, Icilius has found out about Appius's approach to Virginia and confronts him; Appius pleads innocence, suggesting that any letters purporting to come from him have been forged. Realising that their initial approach will no longer work, Clodius forms a new plan: to claim legal ownership of Virginia as a slave, and to have his case heard before Appius, who will of course rule in his favour. Icilius, clearly unconvinced of Appius's innocence, informs his kinsmen of what has transpired in his encounter with Appius. In the public market, Clodius claims ownership of Virginia as a bondswoman, and, upon being challenged by Icilius, a trial is arranged to take place in front of Appius. The trial, which features both Virginius and Virginia in slave's clothes and a characteristically loquacious Websterian lawyer, culminates in Virginius killing his daughter rather than giving her up to Appius; he then escapes to the army camp where the soldiers, hearing of his deed, proclaim him general. Virginius returns to Rome, where his army joins with that of Icilius. Appius and Clodius are imprisoned, and sentenced by Virginius to kill themselves. Appius carries out the sentence, but Clodius refuses to do so; Icilius hands him to the public executioner. Rome reverts to an earlier form of government, and Virginius and Ilicius are appointed consuls.

Appius and Virginia is a much more austere play than either *The White Devil* or *The Duchess of Malfi*, even though it shares with those plays an interest in the disruptive effects of feminine agency in a social world which aims to gender power as 'masculine'. But Virginia is a less complex figure than either Vittoria or the Duchess, and the play's consistency of tone marks it as unusual in Webster's oeuvre. Perhaps this is one reason why *Appius and Virginia* has attracted such little critical comment, and why criticism has largely ignored social and cultural issues, focusing instead on the questions of authorship and date. On these matters, the most recent editors follow the consensus as it stood at the end of the twentieth century: that is, that the play is a collaboration between Heywood and Webster, and that it was composed in the 1620s, probably as the last play on which Webster worked. One recent critic, however, has argued against the second of these claims, suggesting that 'the date of 1624 has hitherto been too readily accepted with only weak evidence. The case for a date before 1616, probably around 1608, is much stronger' (Culhane 2004: 301).

Such a date, of course, if accepted, would significantly alter the shape of Webster's career, suggesting that the move to tragedy happens in collaborative mode before the individual experiments, and that the move towards comedy after the individual works is a decisive one. However, Culhane's suggestions have not been universally accepted, and it seems safest to say that many of the details of Webster's collaborative drama – dates, collaborators, numbers of work extant – remain unclear. What is clear is that Webster spent much of his dramatic career writing in collaboration with other dramatists, and that it seems to have been a mode of work with which he was perfectly comfortable.

CHAPTER 3

'Changeable Stuff': *The White Devil*

The latest of what this book refers to as Webster's 'early' collaborative works, the two *Ho* plays, were performed in 1604–5. After that, Webster's writing for the theatre appears to have dried up, and there are a number of possible reasons for this: perhaps the coach-making business occupied a great deal of his time, perhaps (as some critics think) the collaborative drama *Appius and Virginia* does in fact date from this period, or perhaps Webster did write some more plays which have not survived as printed texts, or have not been recorded in documents of the period. What is certain is that when Webster did return to the stage early in 1612, the resultant play, *The White Devil*, captured the expression of a forcefully idiosyncratic way of viewing the world, in a manner that the earlier plays did not. And, although it is this characteristically 'Websterian' vision which has most interested modern critics, the play was a commercial failure in its own day, rushed into print by Webster himself as a result of a poor reception on the stage. This chapter examines the paradox of *The White Devil*, the question of why a play can inspire such opposite and extreme reactions, and aims to evaluate the historical significance of Webster's first tragic masterpiece.

THE WHITE DEVIL: SUMMARY AND ANALYSIS

Dedication

The action of *The White Devil* is complex and convoluted; the poetry equally so. But in both dramatic and literary terms the play achieves a remarkable synthesis of individual moments – even dramatic 'blocks' (see p. 53) – which are spectacular in themselves, but which nevertheless contain the potential for disjunction and distraction. The play as printed opens with an address from the playwright to the reader, in which Webster strikes a famously rebarbative tone. The opening sentence is one of the most famous in what are known as the 'paratexts' of Renaissance drama; that is, information presented at the beginning and end of play-texts, outside the play proper but, as recent criticism has shown, subtly influencing how readers engage with the drama presented to them. Webster's persona is cautious not to appear too presumptuous: he is not, he claims, the first playwright to publish a tragedy (plays were generally seen in the period as a form of dramatic entertainment, rather than literary art), but merely aims to 'challenge to [that is, claim for] myself that liberty, which other men have ta'en before me' (Pro. 1–2). Immediately, however, Webster begins to make claims for the value of the play, arguing that its failure to do well at the Red Bull theatre was because 'it was acted, in so dull a time of winter, presented in so open and black a theatre, that it wanted (that which is the only grace and setting out of a tragedy) a full and understanding auditory' (Pro. 3–6). Each of Webster's charges here is significant. The Red Bull was an outdoor theatre, and so in the 'dull [. . .] time of winter' in London, it would indeed be 'open' [to the elements] and 'black' [lacking artificial lighting]. This was not the only way in which plays could be staged in the London of the early-seventeenth century; the most prestigious of the playing companies, the King's Men, had residence in two theatres. One, the outdoor Globe, was used primarily for summer performances (it could hold more people, and so the summer weather could be turned to a profit), and the other, the indoor Blackfriars, could be used both for more exclusive (and expensive) performances throughout the year, and to stage plays in the winter which would have been played at the Globe in the summer (Webster's own *The Duchess of Malfi* later followed this pattern). Since the Blackfriars was more expensive, it tended to attract audiences who thought of themselves as being of higher social standing than the 'groundlings' at the Globe; when Webster complains that the play 'wanted [that is, lacked] a full and understanding auditory', he may be complaining about the perceived incapacities of the audience as much as the inclemencies of the Winter weather (an interpretation backed up by his claim that 'most of the people that come to that playhouse resemble [. . .] ignorant asses' (Pro. 7–8)). Webster continues to castigate the audience for what he perceives as their failure to appreciate his play: 'should a man present to such an auditory the most sententious tragedy that ever was written [. . .] the breath that comes from the multitude is able to poison it' (Pro. 17–23). Having defended himself against those critics of his dramatic practice, Webster turns to those who attack his mode (and particularly, his speed) of literary composition: 'To those who report I was a long time in finishing this tragedy, I confess I do not write with a goose-quill' (Pro. 26–7). The charge of lacking urgency seems to have stung Webster, and he appropriates for himself the persona of the classical poet Alcestis, claiming that his work may be slow in composition, but will last for longer than the 'hack' work of more rapid composers.

Misogyny and Destruction

All this cannot help but influence the way modern readers engage with the play and, indeed, since the original performance was not a success, the printed version may well have been how many of Webster's contemporaries first experienced *The White Devil*. But the play itself begins, not in the cold, dark world of early modern London, but in what Webster and many of his peers seem to have regarded as the dazzlingly corrupt and sordid world of Renaissance Italy. The play opens with the banishment from Rome of Count Lodovico, a nobleman who has lived riotously, and instigated violence and murder in the city. Lodovico's speech declaiming his banishment sets the tone for much of what is to follow:

> Ha, ha, O Democritus thy gods
> That govern the whole world! – Courtly reward,
> And punishment! Fortune's a right whore.
> If she give aught, she deals it in small parcels,
> That she may take away all at one swoop.
> This 'tis to have great enemies, God quit them.
> Your wolf no longer seems to be a wolf
> Than when she's hungry. (I, i, 3–9)

Lodovico begins by asserting the social classes – '*courtly* reward' – on which the play will focus. The phrase 'Fortune's a right whore' encapsulates two of Webster's main concerns in the play. Fortune, the guiding goddess of tragedy, is she who is responsible for both the rise and fall of princes and kings (the classical image of Fortune's Wheel is significant in Renaissance theorisations of the tragic genre), while the term 'whore' reverberates throughout this play so concerned with female sexuality, and the perceived social and spiritual dangers thereof. And if femininity is vindictive and corrupt in Lodovico's imagination, it is also animalistic: the wolf in the final two lines is emphatically a she-wolf, hungry and ready to devour. In a very short speech, then, Webster immediately sets in motion a chain of images which will recur with various degrees of force throughout the course of the play.

Other instances of characteristically Websterian imagery also emerge in this opening scene; Gasparo says to Lodovico, 'Your followers have swallowed you like mummia [embalmed flesh, as in a 'mummy'], and being sick [. . .] Vomit you up i'th'kennel' (I, i, 15–18), the emphasis on death and decay here being a favoured bank of imagery for Webster, while the imagery of a sick dog is familiar from a number of Jacobean plays which depict courtly corruption in the image of a 'fawning' dog (most especially, perhaps, those of John Marston, with whom Webster had collaborated on the King's Men version of *The Malcontent*; see pp. 22–3). Similarly, Gasparo's sense that the banishment of Lodovico is a 'gentle penance' (I, i, 36) is just the first example of the language of sin, penitence, and reparation which is found throughout the play in both legal and theological registers.

It falls to Lodovico, the murdering, banished lord, to outline to the audience the relationship which will occupy most of their attention throughout the drama, and it is significant that both parties in the relationship are described in terms which emphasise their similarity to the immoral, banished criminal:

> So, – but I wonder then some great men 'scape
> This banishment. There's Paulo Giordano Orsini,
> The Duke of Bracciano, now lives in Rome,
> And by close pandarism seeks to prostitute
> The honour of Vittoria Corombona–
> Vittoria, she that might have got my pardon
> For one kiss to the duke. (I, i, 39–44)

Thus Vittoria – the titular 'White Devil' – is introduced to the audience through the words of a banished criminal, potentially allied to that criminal in corruption ('she might have got my pardon'), and potentially pandered to a Duke who is distinguishable from that criminal only by virtue of his social standing (his role as one of the 'great men'). For Lodovico, then, Vittoria is doubly damned – by her social position (among the 'great men') and by her gender and sexuality ('she-wolf').

Act One, Scene Two brings Bracciano and Vittoria before the eyes of the audience for the first time, albeit in the company of Camillo, Vittoria's husband, and Flamineo, Bracciano's secretary and Vittoria's brother. Almost immediately, Camillo and Vittoria exit, and Bracciano and Flamineo are left alone on stage. Flamineo's role as the go-between for Bracciano and Vittoria becomes clear: 'The fair Vittoria, my happy sister, / Shall give you present audience', he says to the duke (I, ii, 5–6). Having made such a promise to Bracciano, Flamineo next converses with Camillo, ridiculing him to the audience as 'an ass in's foot-cloth' (I, ii, 51). The conversation turns to the subject of Camillo's and Vittoria's relationship, and Camillo reveals that 'I do not well remember, I protest, / When last I lay with her' (I, ii, 55–6), a confession which affords Flamineo ample opportunity for punning of a sexual nature (I, ii, 57–113), thus building on the atmosphere of corrupted sexuality outlined through the figure of Lodovico. Camillo, it becomes clear, suspects Bracciano of either attempting to seduce Vittoria, or of having already succeeded in his attempt. Again the language in this scene, particularly that of Flamineo, draws attention to two of Webster's preoccupations in both of his major tragedies, the questions of female sexuality and of female confinement or imprisonment:

> Bar your wife of her entertainment; women are more willingly and more gloriously chaste when they are least restrained of their liberty [. . .] These politic enclosures for paltry mutton makes more rebellion in the flesh than all the provocative electuaries doctors have uttered since last Jubilee. (I, ii, 90–7)

In other words, Flamineo here reverses the conventional misogynist wisdom that female chastity can be controlled (by men) by female confinement. There is a pun here on 'liberty', as it can mean 'sexual licentiousness' in the period; thus the juxtaposition of 'chaste' and 'liberty' is on one level a paradox. But the plea for female 'liberty' in a more broadly social, less overtly sexual, sense is not to be understood as suggesting that Flamineo outlines an anti-misogynist viewpoint. On the contrary, his sense of women as 'paltry mutton' makes this clear. In fact, Flamineo is a notoriously unreliable speaker, shifting his opinions depending on his audience, and conscious of his role-playing throughout; he is, as many of the characters in the play are, constantly shifting between performed roles. (Webster's aesthetic relativism here comes close to suggesting one of the insights developed by late-twentieth-century theorists of identity: that 'the self' is often constituted through the act of performance. The performance of social interaction *constructs*, rather than *reveals*, the self.) This becomes even clearer when Vittoria re-enters, and Flamineo speaks to her in asides, unable to be heard by Camillo: 'I must now *seemingly* fall out with you' (I, ii, 129–30; italics mine). Vittoria joins in the pretence: when Flamineo is apparently trying to persuade her to go to bed with Camillo, she says to him, aside: 'How shall's rid him hence?' (I, ii, 161), the 'us' in 'shall's' establishing the conspiratorial tone between the siblings. The objective of both is achieved by Flamineo, drawing on the misogyny that he has earlier planted in the mind of Camillo, urging him to think that women are solely driven by their passions (particularly their sexual ones); thus Camillo vows that 'for this night I would not lie with her, I would cross her humour to make her more humble' (I, ii, 166–7). Flamineo and Vittoria thereby achieve their aim of ensuring that Camillo stays apart from Vittoria for that night. With Camillo off-stage, Flamineo addresses Vittoria in terms which suggest that his misogyny might be more deep-seated than purely strategic:

> Come sister, darkness hides your blush. Women are like curst dogs: civility keeps them tied all daytime, but they are let loose at midnight; then they do most good or mischief. (I, ii, 199–202)

Again the imagery linking female sexuality, restraint, and animalistic behaviour recurs here.

At this point, Bracciano re-enters, and a carpet and cushions are laid on stage for his seduction of Vittoria. This is one of many 'set-pieces' in the play (the trial of Vittoria is the most famous) which both heighten the dramatic effectiveness, yet simultaneously call attention to the 'constructed' nature of the piece. Unknown to the other characters, however, the seduction scene is witnessed and overheard by Cornelia, the mother of Vittoria and Flamineo (metatheatrically acknowledging the presence of the theatre audience). Bracciano's speech of seduction begins as a stilted attempt at persuasion, a parody by Webster of such speeches, at which Bracciano is comically inept:

> Let me into your bosom, happy lady,
> Pour out instead of eloquence my vows. –
> Loose me not madam, for if you forgo me
> I am lost eternally. (I, ii, 206–9)

Bracciano's lack of eloquence is clear throughout, both in this speech and in the rather clumsy punning on the exchange of 'jewels' (meaning both jewellery and chastity or honour). The longest speeches of the scene, however, go to the charismatic Vittoria, whose control of language, both as a rhetorical ornament, and as a means to instigate action, are clearest in her relation of her 'dream' to Bracciano (I, ii, 233–56); whereas Bracciano's speeches are composed of ineloquent wooing and clumsy punning, Vittoria provides a studiedly ambiguous narrative. This means that Bracciano and Flamineo's interpretation of the dream – 'She hath taught him in a dream / To make away his duchess and her husband', as Flamineo puts it – is never explicitly acknowledged as truthful by Vittoria (who is, even at this point, perhaps thinking of the legal and theological implications of unguarded speech; it might then be especially significant that Bracciano promises to seat Vittoria 'above law and above scandal' (I, ii, 264)).

Appearing to move towards a resolution, the scene moves to confrontation again when Cornelia makes her presence known. In addition to giving a voice to conventional morality – she is dismayed at what she has witnessed – Cornelia also has an important plot function, insofar as she makes the main characters aware of the next impediment to their plan, the arrival in Rome of Bracciano's wife, the duchess Isabella. Vittoria, hit by the double blow of Isabella's arrival and Cornelia's curse, exits the stage, exclaiming 'O me accurst!' (I, ii, 301–2). Bracciano, enraged, accuses Cornelia of raising 'a fearful and prodigious storm' (I, ii, 307) ('storm' here drawing attention to another significant cluster of imagery in the play), before exiting to leave Flamineo and Cornelia alone on stage. In the ensuing discussion between the two, Flamineo ascribes his behaviour to his poverty (holding Cornelia responsible for that poverty) – 'I would fain know where lies the mass of wealth / Which you have hoarded for my inheritance', he sarcastically proclaims (I, ii, 312–13) – while Cornelia again adopts the viewpoint of a conventional morality: 'What? Because we are poor, / Shall we be vicious?' (I, ii, 315–16). The exchange results in another outburst of misogyny from Flamineo, using the language of prostitution to describe all women, even his own mother:

> I would the common'st courtesan in Rome
> Had been my mother rather than thyself.
> Nature is very pitiful to whores
> To give them but few children, yet those children
> Plurality of fathers; they are sure
> They will not want. (I, ii, 335–40)

By this stage of the play, then, the word 'whore' and its associated misogynistic discourse have been firmly established as one of the materials with which Webster is constructing his play. In an even more self-referential mode, Flamineo's words which close the act have been taken by many critics as an apt metaphor for the convoluted dramaturgy which follows in the rest of the play:

> We are engaged to mischief and must on.
> As rivers to find out the ocean
> Flow with crook bendings beneath forcéd banks,
> Or as we see, to aspire some mountain's top,
> The way ascends not straight, but imitates
> The subtle foldings of a winter's snake,
> So who knows policy and her true aspect,
> Shall find her ways winding and indirect. (I, ii, 348–55)

As if to back up Flamineo's point about the 'winding and indirect' unfolding of the narrative, Act Two opens with a host of characters whom the audience has not previously witnessed on stage, although Webster's 'subtle foldings' are such that some of them have already played an important part in absentia. The audience is presented with Francisco de Medici (the Duke of Florence), the Cardinal Monticelso, Marcello (brother to Flamineo and Vittoria, and employed in the household of Francisco), Isabella (Bracciano's wife), and Isabella and Bracciano's young son Giovanni. The initial action of the scene is a discussion between Isabella and Francisco, both of whom are keen for Bracciano to return to his wife and son (Isabella and Francisco are siblings). Significantly, even Isabella, the character most in keeping with the early modern stereotype of an obedient and faithful wife, seems linguistically contaminated by the corruption of the play-world, describing her wifely embraces in the language of witchcraft:

> As men to try the precious unicorn's horn
> Make of the powder a preservative circle
> And in it put a spider, so these arms
> Shall charm his poison, force it to obeying
> And keep him chaste from an infected straying. (II, i, 14–18)

This is also, of course, another instance of the play's phobic insistence on the (sexualised) power of women to control men. Isabella exits before Bracciano enters to begin his conversation with Francisco and Monticelso: thus the dramaturgy makes the gendered structures of power in Webster's Italy clear to the audience. With the three men alone on stage, Francisco and Monticelso castigate Bracciano for his abandonment of Isabella and pursuit of Vittoria: again the language employed is that of a misogynistic discourse on female sexuality, comparing Vittoria to a 'lascivious dream', a 'dunghill bird', a 'strumpet', a 'whore', a 'wild duck' (slang for a prostitute), all the time reinforcing the equation between female sexuality and a base, animalistic materialism. Bracciano makes no attempt to deny his pursuit of Vittoria, and both his challenge to Francisco – 'All thy loud cannons and thy borrowed Switzers, / Thy galleys, nor thy sworn confederates, / Durst not supplant her' (II, i, 61–3) – and Francisco's reply – 'would I had given / Both [Isabella's] white hands to death, bound and locked fast / In her last winding-sheet' (II, i, 64–6) – assert again the link made by the play between illicit sexuality and violence and death. When Giovanni enters, Monticelso attempts to use the relationship which both men have with the boy (he is, of course, Bracciano's son and Francisco's nephew), but even this attempt at reconciliation is couched in the imagery of storms and tempests which represent political and dynastic quarrels throughout the play: 'Leave him a stock of virtue that may last, / Should fortune rend his sails and split his mast' (II, i, 106–7; note again the dangers inherent in *The White Devil*'s sense of 'fortune'; see pp. 34–5). Some light-hearted banter with Giovanni does, indeed, calm the situation, and Francisco and Bracciano agree that 'you and I are friends' (II, i, 139), although the audience surely remains aware that no solution to the initial quarrel has been forthcoming. Isabella re-enters, and the Duke and Cardinal exit to leave the husband and wife onstage together for the first time in the play. The ensuing discussion reveals Isabella's patient devotion to her husband, which of course is not matched by Bracciano, who rejects her pleas for a reunion, urging instead that 'I'll ne'er more lie with thee' (II, i, 195); this recalls to the audience Camillo's confession to Flamineo in Act One, but is clearly amplified to a greater degree here. Bracciano's informal 'divorce' will be treated, he claims, as an official one would: 'this divorce shall be as truly kept / As if the judge had doomed [that is, pronounced] it' (II, i, 196–7). Isabella, fearing the enmity which might arise between Bracciano and Francisco, resolves to inform the latter that the 'divorce' occurred at her instigation alone. True to her word, when Francisco and Monticelso re-enter, Isabella rails against Bracciano and, in an out-burst which is partly role-play, but which may also be calculated by Webster to display a deeper frustration within the character, against Vittoria:

> To dig the strumpet's eyes out, let her lie
> Some twenty months a–dying, to cut off
> Her nose and lips, pull out her rotten teeth,
> Preserve her flesh like mummia, for trophies
> Of my just anger! (II, i, 246–50)

As in the frequent misogynistic outbursts against female sexuality, the body of Vittoria is once again foregrounded here, the language of illicit sex ('strumpet') alongside the imagery of bodily death and decay (and the image of the mummy, recalling, of course, the earlier use of that image to describe the other 'outsider', Lodovico, in Act One; see p. 35). Isabella exits just before the entrance of Camillo, who is on stage (but not part of the conversation) when Flamineo, Bracciano and a 'stock' doctor are discussing their plan to murder Camillo and Isabella. After the exit of the conspirators, Camillo is approached by Francisco and Monticelso, who inform him of rumours that he is being cuckolded, give him a commission to challenge pirates around the Italian coast, and tell him that they will spy on Vittoria in his absence. The commission is a fabrication: Lodovico, the banished lord from the beginning of the play, is no longer involved in piracy, but is instead aiming to ingratiate his way back into courtly society. Francisco and Monticelso, having arranged the absence of Camillo, turn their attention to the plan to catch Bracciano red-handed in his adultery with Vittoria; 'I fain would have the Duke Bracciano run / Into notorious scandal', claims Francisco (II, i, 386–7). The scene closes with Francisco employing a characteristically Websterian image linking sexuality and decay: 'Like mistletoe on sere [i.e., withered] elms spent by weather, / Let him cleave to her and both rot together' (II, i, 397–8).

Vittoria's Trial

After the long scene of Act Two, Scene One, Webster's dramaturgy changes abruptly, in one of the most extreme examples of his aesthetic relativism; Act Two, Scene Two is a short scene which delivers its message through the Renaissance dramatic convention of the 'dumb show', a dramatic moment whereby gestures, rather than speech, are made to carry the weight of the scene's communicative function. Establishing a dialogue between the representational and non-representational aspects of his art, Webster makes his dumb shows serve a function within the narrative (they are visions presented to Bracciano by a conjurer) and within the drama (they quickly summarise key plot events for the audience). Although the conjurer, who appears only in this scene, is clearly a dramatic device to enable Bracciano's vision, nevertheless his presence on stage adds to the atmosphere of subterfuge throughout the play, in addition to giving a more concrete form to the supernatural (particularly diabolic) imagery deployed throughout, from the title onwards. The first dumb show reveals the death of Isabella, who has been killed by kissing a picture of Bracciano, poisoned by the doctor who appeared on stage in the preceding scene. The second, more complicated, dumb show represents the death of Camillo, who has been killed by Flamineo in an incident designed to appear like a sporting accident. The audience learn that Flamineo and Marcello have been arrested, and that Francisco and Monticelso are on their way to arrest Vittoria as well.

In the time imagined to pass between Act Two and Act Three, Vittoria has evidently been arrested, as Act Three, Scene One opens with the preparations for her trial. Francisco and Monticelso, knowing that 'we have nought but circumstances / To charge her with' (III, i, 4–5), have arranged the presence of the various ambassadors resident in Rome, so that 'the proofs / Of her black lust shall make her infamous / To all our neighbouring kingdoms' (III, i, 6–8). Meanwhile, Flamineo again outlines his motivation for his course of action – 'how shall we find reward?' (III, i, 49) – while Marcello is shown to be very much on the same moralistic side as his mother – 'I would my dagger's point had cleft [Vittoria's] heart / When she first saw Bracciano' (III, i, 33–4) – thus reinforcing to the audience the familial division occasioned by the play's events.

Act Three, Scene Two is arguably the centre of the play, a status reinforced by the very unusual way in which the scene is given a title ('The Arraignment of Vittoria') in the earliest printed edition. To the surprise of the characters on stage, Bracciano arrives to witness the trial; with no place reserved for him, he is forced to spread his cloak on the floor and sit on that. The trial begins with a lawyer speaking in Latin; Vittoria objects, claiming that 'amongst this auditory / Which come to hear my cause, the half or more / May be ignorant in't' (III, ii, 15–17). In contrast, Monticelso suggests that Vittoria may not wish the accusations to be widely known: 'gentlewoman, your credit / Shall be more famous by it' (III, ii, 22–3). Vittoria, however, maintains her protest, and the lawyer is forced to speak in English; when his English is almost as Latinate as his Latin ('Exorbitant sins must have exculceration', III, ii, 34), Vittoria again objects: 'Why, this is Welsh to Latin [i.e. incomprehensible]' III, ii, 39). The lawyer is dismissed from the court, which leaves Monticelso to put the case against Vittoria, a duality of function which is not ignored by the woman on trial: 'It doth not suit a reverend cardinal / To play the lawyer thus' (III, ii, 60–1); 'If you be my accuser, / Pray cease to be my judge' (III, ii, 225–6). Monticelso's stated aim – to be 'plainer' than the lawyer (III, ii, 51) – results in a much more emotive and accusatory language, with the words 'whore' and 'devil' echoing throughout his speeches (III, ii, 56, 69, 77ff., 108–10). Particularly vituperative is the 'perfect character' of a whore speech (III, ii, 78–101), which gives a rhetorically dense and elaborate series of metaphors for sexual licentiousness. Attempting to blame Vittoria for the death of her husband, Francisco and Monticelso increasingly resort to personal attacks, including criticising the appearance of Vittoria – 'She comes not like a widow; she comes armed / With scorn and impudence. Is this a mourning habit?' (III, ii, 119–21). Vittoria's defence, that the pressures placed on her by the court are wresting her away from conventionally feminine behaviour and thus should not be seen as a sign of guilt, is eloquently and forcefully put: '[I am] So entangled in a cursèd accusation, / That my defence, of force like Perseus [killer of Medusa], / Must personate masculine virtue' (III, ii, 134–6). Perseus, in Greek myth, was the slayer of Medusa, the snake-haired Gorgon whom Renaissance authorities often saw as an image of the monstrosity of female sexuality and/or power. Thus Vittoria reverses gendered stereotypes here, associating her accusers, with their entangling curses, with Medusa, while she represents the masculine force of Perseus. Although the strategy is rhetorically effective, it nevertheless leaves unchallenged the patriarchal assumption that 'virtue' must always be considered as a 'masculine' state. Thus, the final gendering of 'virtue' draws attention to the differing demands placed on men and women by the world of Renaissance Italy (and, by implication, by the world of Jacobean England outside the playhouse walls). Continuing with her strategy, applying the bodily imagery attached to sexuality throughout the play to her accusers, Vittoria emphatically rejects the roles which have been ascribed to her:

> Terrify, babes, my lord, with painted devils;
> I am past such needless palsy. For your names
> Of whore and murd'ress, they proceed from you,
> As if a man should spit against the wind,
> The filth returns in's face. (III, ii, 147–51)

Here Vittoria rejects the appellations which have been forced on her by the masculine society of the play ('devil', 'whore', 'murd'ress'), with an image of the hostility and 'filth' of the 'natural' world (she is like 'the wind', returning the terms to the accusers). It is at this, emotionally charged, point that Bracciano makes his presence in the courtroom felt, and begins to answer some of the accusations levelled at Vittoria. However, Bracciano is made of less stern stuff than Vittoria, and after a couple of heated exchanges with Monticelso, he leaves the courtroom (an option, of course, which is not available to Vittoria). Perhaps fearing, as he has already suggested, that there is insufficient evidence to convict Vittora of murder, Francisco suggests to Monticelso that he aim for the lesser conviction of adultery; this change raises the suspicions of Vittoria, who employs another of the play's characteristic image-sets, that of sickness, medication and disease: 'I discern poison / Under your gilded pills' (III, ii, 190–1; see also III, ii, 276–7; here, as throughout, the images call attention to the frailty and corruptibility of the body). On this charge, too, Vittoria draws attention to the lack of evidence linking her to the accusation:

> Sum up my faults, I pray, and you shall find
> That beauty and gay clothes, a merry heart,
> And a good stomach to a feast, are all,
> All the poor crimes that you can charge me with. (III, ii, 207–10)

It would have been clear to a Jacobean audience that Vittoria is here rejecting the Renaissance stereotype of the silent and obedient wife, but also that the rejection of that stereotype is not in itself sufficient justification for standing trial (the complicating factor, of course, is that Vittoria *is* guilty of adultery and of plotting murder, and thus her pleas are as empty and as hypocritical as are those of her accusers; thus Vittoria occupies an ethically and legally problematic position throughout this scene). Monticelso, by now struggling to cope with Vittoria's robust defence, returns to his earlier strategy of imputing sinfulness to the defendant: 'If the devil / Did ever take good shape, behold his picture' (III, ii, 216–17); 'You came from thence a most notorious strumpet, / And so you have continued' (III, ii, 244–5). He continues by suggesting that Vittoria's sinfulness is public knowledge – 'I make but repetition / Of what is ordinary and Rialto talk' (III, ii, 247–8) – thus implying that the trial itself is unnecessary since its outcome is not in doubt. As such, Monticelso moves quickly to sentencing Vittoria, despite her resistance to the charges throughout: she is sent to 'a house of convertites . . . a house of penitent whores' (III, ii, 266–7). As the scene draws on earlier parallels between sexuality and social control, so too Vittoria expresses the corruption of the law as a sexual violation: 'A rape, a rape [. . .] you have ravished justice, / Forced her to do your pleasure' (III, ii, 274–5). One effect of the employment of this imagery, of course, is to call into question the assumption made between masculinity and virtue: as an emphatically gender-specific crime, rape portrays masculine identity in its most vicious aspect. Yet despite this outburst, Vittoria is carried off to her punishment. At this point, Bracciano re-enters, acts strangely, and leaves: Flamineo correctly identifies this as a sign that Isabella is dead. The rest of the characters become aware of this through the entrance of Giovanni, mourning the loss of his mother. Distressed, Giovanni's speeches ('What do the dead do, uncle? Do they eat, / Hear music, go a-hunting, and be merry, / As we that live?', III, ii, 324–6), draw attention to another of the key concerns of Webster's tragic period, namely the memorialisation of the dead and their deeds and qualities. The scene thus ends with Francisco vowing to perform the significant Websterian role of the living memorial:

> Believe me, I am nothing but her grave,
> And I shall keep her blessèd memory
> Longer than thousand epitaphs. (III, ii, 342–4)

Ritual and Vengeance

Act Three, Scene Three has two main dramatic functions: to continue the narrative of Flamineo's sense of disenfranchisement and corresponding melancholic character; and to stage for the audience the return of the banished count Lodovico to the aristocratic circles of the play's main plot.

Act Four, Scene One, meanwhile, begins with another scene of private conference between Francisco and Monticelso. Both men are aware of the role played by Bracciano in murdering Isabella (Francisco's sister, of course, as well as Bracciano's wife), and both are keen that some kind of revenge is in order; at this point, the similarities between *The White Devil* and the popular Renaissance genre of revenge tragedy begin to become more apparent, although the structure of *The White Devil* always resists the full generic condition of revenge tragedy. Act Four, Scene Two takes place at the House of Convertites where Vittoria is imprisoned. Bracciano resolves to arrange Vittoria's escape from the house of convertites; the political unrest in Rome, where the pope has died and a successor has yet to be elected, is identified by Flamineo as a propitious context for staging such an escape. The scene ends with Flamineo again dissatisfied with his lot, feeling that he must work towards Bracciano's plan to escape from Rome and unite in Padua, but resentful that 'Knaves do grow great by being great men's apes' (IV, ii, 249).

Act Four, Scene Three allows Webster to represent onstage the ritual aspects of Roman Catholicism so fascinating to Jacobean audiences, while at the same time confirming the prejudices of those audiences that the theatricality of Roman ritual is an index of immoral hypocrisy. Although both Lodovico and Francisco are present on stage as the scene begins, and the audience is clearly expecting some interaction between the two, the initial business of the scene is to stage the parade of ambassadors, the rituals of papal election, and the installation of Cardinal Monticelso as the new pope, Paul IV. The scene lurches back towards the main plot of the play when Monticelso uses his new-found powers to excommunicate Bracciano and Vittoria on finding out about their escape. After Monticelso leaves the stage, the expected moment of conspiracy between Francisco and Lodovico takes place, the former revealing that the latter has 'ta'en the sacrament to prosecute / Th'intended murder' (IV, iii, 72–3). This refers to the act of swearing on the consecrated bread of the eucharist; clearly, swearing to perform a murder is a violation of the spiritual significance of the Catholic ritual. Immediately afterwards, Lodovico is confronted by Monticelso, who urges him to abandon the plan to murder Bracciano (Lodovico reveals the plan under the confessional, a characteristically Roman Catholic practice, the reference to which furthers Webster's strategy of presenting Catholicism as an exotic and corrupt form of religious practice). Lodovico, surprised at the reluctance of Monticelso to approve the murder, wavers in his resolve, but the arrival of a sum of money, in reality sent by Francisco but purporting to come from Monticelso, convinces him that the new pope has simply been 'politic' in his dealings, and strengthens his determination to see the murder through. As the act ends, Lodovico utters the ominous warning, 'Now to th'act of blood' (IV, iii, 151), a self-referential use of the language of dramatic construction ('act') which also, given the religious context of the scene, draws an ironic parallel between the sacrifice of Christ's blood in the sacrament, and the spiritually empty bloodletting which is to follow.

Act Five moves the location of the action to Bracciano's court in Padua; the first scene opens with an elaborate procession over the stage, recalling, perhaps, the ambassadorial and papal ritual of Rome, but signalling to the audience that Bracciano and Vittoria have successfully escaped to Padua and are now married. Flamineo remains on stage with Bracciano's servant Hortensio, and the conversation between the two allows the audience to catch up on the action which has taken place between the acts. Webster uses this dialogue to introduce what appear to be new characters, 'the Moor that's come to court' (V, i, 4) (Mulinassar, who is actually Francisco in disguise), and 'Two noblemen of Hungary [. . .] entered into religion, into the strict order of Capuchins' (V, i, 13–16; in reality Lodovico and his acquaintance from the opening scene, Gasparo). The disguised characters enter, are accepted into the society of the court by Bracciano, but then renew their conspiracy against the Duke. After the conspiracy is made known to the audience, Francisco remains on stage, to be encountered by Flamineo, who believes him to be the Moor Mulinassar. They begin by discussing the ('really') Moorish woman Zanche, a servant of Vittoria's, who is erotically engaged with Flamineo, but will later shift her affections towards Francisco (again believing him to be Mulinassar). Francisco and Flamineo discuss the merits (or otherwise) of being a solider, Flamineo rejecting the trials of the field for the corruption (sexual and political) of the court: 'Give me a fair room yet hung with arras, and some great cardinal to lug me by th'ears as his endeared minion [lover]' (V, i, 122–4). Having established the reputation of Mulinassar as a soldier and man of action, Francisco exits; Zanche enters, and at this point the audience become aware of the relationship between her and Flamineo: 'I do love that Moor, that witch, very constrainedly' (V, i, 152–3). The scene is interrupted by the appearance of Cornelia (Flamineo and Vittoria's mother), who attacks Zanche; she is joined by Marcello, who kicks Zanche. Flamineo displays a certain anger at the violence directed towards Zanche, but Cornelia and Marcello are consistent in their opposition to the relationship: 'If I take her near you I'll cut her throat', says Marcello (V, i, 200). Amid much discord, all the characters exit except Zanche, leaving her alone on stage to greet the reappearance of the disguised Francisco. Zanche attempts to seduce

Francisco; the latter sees this as an opportunity to gain 'intelligence [secret information]' (V, i, 233), and the two exit together.

Act Five, Scene Two is a short scene, but an important one both in moving Flamineo further towards the role of murderous malcontent, and in moving the play itself further towards its bloody conclusion. The scene opens with a moment of familial intimacy between Cornelia and Marcello, lamenting the decline of their family's fortunes, and remembering the moment in the family's past when Flamineo broke Cornelia's crucifix, an event which Marcello predicted as an omen of ill events to come. Although Elizabeth Williamson has recently argued that the crucifix is here to be understood primarily as a domestic, rather than a religious, object, it seems that the religious context is entirely appropriate. By breaking the crucifix, Flamineo breaks (again) the body of Christ; this foreshadows the bloody closure of the play and, in addition to the staging of Catholic spectacle in Act Four, Scene Three (see pp. 47–8), encourages the audience to view the play's bloody end as a perversion of Catholic ritual. Anticipating the events to come, Flamineo enters and immediately murders his brother, resulting in Cornelia's distraction and near-madness. Attempting to escape, Flamineo is apprehended by Bracciano and the disguised Flamineo. Cornelia draws her knife to kill Flamineo, but changes her mind at the last minute, unable to face the death of another son. Bracciano grants Flamineo a pardon, which must be renewed at the end of every day. Meanwhile, the conspiracy to kill Bracciano gathers pace, as the disguised Lodovico, with the full knowledge of the disguised Francisco, poisons the helmet of Bracciano's armour.

Act Five, Scene Three continues the play's move towards a chaotic spectacle of death. The scene opens with another moment of ritualised display, recalling the dumb shows of Bracciano's visions, the election of the Pope, and the marriage of Bracciano and Vittoria. The event this time is a duelling tournament (the reason, of course, why Bracciano needs his armour). After a few duels have been staged, it becomes clear that the poison on Bracciano's helmet is beginning to have an effect, as he calls for the helmet to be removed: 'my brain's on fire' (V, iii, 4). Bracciano, of course, realises who has poisoned him: 'this unction is sent from the great Duke of Florence' (V, iii, 27; on the significance of the term 'unction', see below). Rehearsing one of the central concerns of the play, Bracciano suggests that unnatural deaths are a result of the scheming and manipulation of the corrupt courtly society:

> O thou soft natural death, that art joint-twin
> To sweetest slumber, no rough-bearded comet
> Stares on thy mild departure; the dull owl
> Beats not against thy casement; the hoarse wolf
> Scents not thy carrion. Pity winds thy corse,
> Whilst horror waits on princes. (V, iii, 29–34)

Owls and wolves, of course, are associated throughout this play with the corruption of the aristocratic classes but also with women: it is thus significant that Bracciano locates his death ''Mongst women howling!' (V, iii, 37). The Websterian interest in Catholic ritual comes through again at this point, as Lodovico and Gasparo, disguised of course as Capuchin monks, enter, ostensibly to perform the sacrament of extreme unction, one of the Catholic 'last rites' for the dying. They take Bracciano off-stage, where the ritual can be performed in private. After a suitable interval, during which Flamineo again outlines his characteristic cynicism towards the courtly life, Bracciano, on his dying bed and with Vittoria by his side, is brought back on stage. By now, the poison is evidently working its way into Bracciano's brain and he appears confused and distracted, even claiming to have a vision of the devil (emphasising again, of course, the diabolic imagery central to the play's construction). As he appears near death, the disguised Lodovico and Gasparo begin their ritual, with a crucifix (recalling Cornelia's broken crucifix), a candle, and the use of Latin; when Bracciano is unable to speak any more, Lodovico and Gasparo ask the other characters to leave, and then reveal their identity to the dying Duke. Their taunting and verbal torment of Bracciano is interrupted when the Duke regains the power of speech, calling for Vittoria, who is immediately ushered off-stage before she can witness what is happening; Bracciano is then strangled by Lodovico. Vittoria's grief at the death of Bracciano is, characteristically, dismissed by the cynical Flamineo as 'moonish [i.e., changeable, like the moon] shades of griefs or fears' (V, iii, 186). With Bracciano's death

accomplished, the attention of Francisco is turned again towards
Zanche, who re-enters with a warning that she has had a porten-
tous dream. At this point, Zanche reveals the 'intelligence' which
Francisco has been seeking:

> . . . I did tell you
> I would reveal a secret. Isabella,
> The Duke of Florence' sister, was empoisoned
> By a 'fumed picture; and Camillo's neck
> Was broke by damned Flamineo; the mischance
> Laid on a vaulting horse. (V, iii, 243–8)

Francisco thus becomes aware of the narrative which has been
withheld from him. Conscious of her culpability, Zanche now plots
to make her escape from the court.

Act Five, Scene Four begins with an encounter between
Giovanni and Flamineo, in which the latter encourages the former
to leave mourning and accept the responsibilities thrust on him by
his father's death. Giovanni, ominously for Flamineo, reacts coldly
to his advice, and seeks to have him removed from the presence.
The scene moves to reveal – another ritual moment – the funeral
procession of Marcello's corpse, with Cornelia, Zanche, and other
ladies singing and weeping. The hint of madness in Cornelia's
previous appearance is now magnified as the mother is shown to be
distracted with grief. It is the sight of his mother in such distress
which finally appears to crack the cynical casing of Flamineo: 'I
have a strange thing in me, to th'which / I cannot give a name,
without it be / Compassion' (V, iv, 114–16). Alone on stage, this
translates into an even more astonishing admission of guilt:

> . . . I have lived
> Riotously ill, like some that live in court;
> And sometimes, when my face was full of smiles,
> Have felt the maze of conscience in my breast. (V, iv, 119–22)

It is at just this moment of remorse that the ghost of Bracciano
enters to Flamineo. Unlike some of the other visions in the play,
Flamineo seems convinced that this is a real apparition, and not

just a vision caused by melancholy: 'In what place art thou? In yon starry gallery, / Or in the cursèd dungeon?' (V, iv, 128–9). Flamineo is now nearing the distraction shared by his mother, but whereas Cornelia's was caused by grief, the overriding emotion driving Flamineo at this point seems to be a conflicted sense of guilt. Even at this point in the play, however, Webster calls attention to his authorial presence, and to the aesthetic relativism which is his guiding principle. For if the play presents itself as constructed from a series of dramatic 'blocks' – a seduction scene, a trial scene, a supernatural dumb-show – then this moment audaciously appropriates elements of an existing play: both Cornelia's distraction and the appearance of Bracciano's ghost seem explicitly designed to call to mind similar moments in Shakespeare's *Hamlet*, specifically the madness of Ophelia, and the ghost of Old Hamlet.

Act Five, Scene Five is a very short scene, which displays a conspiratorial moment being overheard for the first time in the play (the conspirators are Francisco and Lodovico, the listener Hortensio, Bracciano's servant). Act Five, Scene Six brings Vittoria back on stage, this time carrying a book, a conventional sign of either devotion or of melancholy. Flamineo has come to her to determine what his status will be in the court, now under the sway of Vittoria following the death of the Duke. Vittoria refuses to grant him any reward: 'You are a villain' (V, vi, 16). Flamineo, enraged, exits and re-enters with two pistols. Vittoria tries to prevent their use by expounding a conventional Christian doctrine to Flamineo, but his guilt and remorse appear to have left him at this moment, as he returns to the irreligious attitude glanced elsewhere in the play:

> Leave your prating,
> For these are but grammatical laments,
> Feminine arguments, and they move me
> As some in pulpits move their auditory
> More with their exclamation than sense
> Of reason, or sound doctrine. (V, vi, 67–72)

Vittoria (and Zanche, who is already being threatened with death) change approach, and suggest that they will kill Flamineo and then kill themselves; he appears to accept this plan. They shoot, and Flamineo falls; Vittoria and Zanche, of course, refuse to carry out the rest of the plan to kill themselves, even when the apparently dying Flamineo wills them to. However, the pistols were not loaded, and Flamineo rises to his feet again; the betrayal by Vittoria and Zanche gives him another opportunity to engage in misogynistic outbursts: 'Trust a woman? – Never, never [. . .] For one Hypermnestra that saved her lord and husband, forty-nine of her sisters cut their husbands' throats all in one night' (V, vi, 160–5). On hearing the cries of Vittoria, Lodovico and Gasparo enter, and reveal their disguises to Flamineo; Flamineo and Vittoria realise that they will both be killed. The first to die is Zanche, killed by both Lodovico and Gasparo. While Flamineo prepares to accept his death in his characteristically cynical fashion, Vittoria is affected more deeply by the prospect of dying: 'My soul, like to a ship in a black storm, / Is driven I know not whither' (V, vi, 248–9). Vittoria dies first, followed soon afterwards by Flamineo. The ambassadors and Giovanni enter too late to save Vittoria and Flamineo but they shoot as they enter, wounding Lodovico; he and the other conspirators are taken away to prison and torture. Lodovico, unrepentant to the end, accepts responsibility for the multiple deaths, displays pride in his achievement, and welcomes his punishment:

> . . . For my part,
> The rack, the gallows, and the torturing wheel
> Shall be but sound sleeps to me. Here's my rest;
> I limbed [painted] this night-piece [night-scene] and it was
>   my best.
>
> (V, vi, 294–7)

If Lodovico's delight in destruction marks him as the villain of the piece, nevertheless his equal delight in a quasi-artistic *construction* of the scene reveals him to be, on one level, a mouthpiece for Webster himself. The task of restoring order to the state by uttering the final words of the play, however, falls to the young Giovanni, the heir to the dukedom; but given what has immediately preceded, his final couplet – 'Let guilty men remember their black deeds / Do lean on crutches, made of slender reeds' (V, vi, 300–1) – seems entirely inadequate. The play thus ends on a profoundly pessimistic note, supported by the fact that Francisco – the most senior aristocratic figure in the play – has escaped punishment.

CRITICAL HISTORY

Early Responses

If Webster's prologue to the reader is to be believed, then *The White Devil* was unpopular with its earliest audiences; his apparent rushing of the play into print could be seen as an attempt to establish it as a text for reading, rather than witnessing (in his introduction to *The Duchess of Malfi*, Webster appears to make a distinction between the 'poem' – the longer, fuller version of the text, more suitable for reading – and the 'presentment' – the theatrical version of the text, shortened for performance). It is unfortunately very hard to tell what the earliest reading audiences made of the play, as little comment survives. The few seventeenth-century responses to Webster which have come down to us do suggest that the play as printed may have remained more popular then the play as performed, but the references are so few that it is impossible to generalise. In 1650, one Abraham Wright recorded in his commonplace book (a book intended for private reference, in which the author noted down phrases or insights that seemed important, thus preserving them for later use), a distinction between the play as read and as performed, albeit one that reverses the earlier audience response; for Wright, *The White Devil* is 'but an indifferent play to read, but for the presentments I believe good' (Moore 1981: 33). The closest Wright gets to literary criticism of the play is in terse comment, 'The lines are too much rhyming' (Moore 1981: 33) which, despite its brevity, anticipates later negative responses to Webster's characteristic use of moral *sententiae*. A much more enthusiastic response, composed around the same time, came from the Presbyterian-turned-Royalist writer, Samuel Sheppard, in his *Epigrams Theological, Philosophical, and Romantic* (1651). Addressing Webster directly, Sheppard's praise is effusive:

'How pretty are thy lines, thy Verses stand / Like unto precious Jewels set in gold, / And grace thy fluent Prose' (Moore 1981: 133). Having praised Webster's literary skills, he goes on to praise his powers of characterisation, before elevating him to the role of a poet for posterity:

> *Vittoria Corombona*, that famed Whore,
> Desperate *Lodovico* weltering in his gore,
> Subtle *Francisco*, all of them shall be,
> Gazed at as Comets by Posterity:
> And thou meantime with never withering Bays,
> Shall Crowned be by all that read thy Layes. (Moore 1981: 134)

Sheppard's image of Webster crowned with bay leaves is a classically-derived image of poetic excellence, and it does seem that Sheppard, writing of course in the midst of the Civil Wars (when the London theatres were closed), views Webster as a poet, rather than as a dramatist. With the Restoration of the monarchy in 1660, and the reopening of the theatres, *The White Devil* was once again staged. The diarist and theatregoer Samuel Pepys, however, was less than taken with the play when he witnessed two performances in October 1661: 'I never had so little pleasure in a play in my life' (Moore 1981: 37). The dissatisfaction displayed by Pepys seems to have been characteristic of his age; when Nahum Tate, four decades later, 'adapted' *The White Devil* to form the basis of his play *Injur'd Love*, readers (it appears not to have been staged) seem to have been completely unaware of Webster's play. And the eighteenth century in general ignored Webster; as the critic Don D. Moore suggests, 'generally speaking, there is no critical heritage of John Webster between 1700 and 1800' (Moore 1981: 5).

Lamb, Hazlitt and the Nineteenth-Century Debates

It was in the nineteenth century, then, that debates over the value of Webster's work begin to re-emerge. A number of individual critics are significant in the nineteenth-century re-evaluation of Webster, among them Charles Lamb and William Hazlitt

(Romantic enthusiasts), Alexander Dyce (the first modern editor of Webster's works) and, resisting many of the claims of these critics, Charles Kingsley and his followers. Criticism of Webster in the nineteenth century focused on a number of key issues, which display both the critics' sense of Webster's art, and the particular interests of their own historical era. Primarily these include the canonisation of Webster as a great artist; the relative significance of dramatic structure and poetic inspiration in *The White Devil*; the 'gothicism' or apparent morbidity of Webster's temperament; and the powers of characterisation on display in the tragedy. All of these can be related to the cultural phenomenon of Romanticism, the privileging of individualism and self-expression over the slavish adherence to rules and formulae: it may be no surprise that the Romantics found in Webster's anti-classical aesthetic relativism a mirroring of their own concerns.

In terms of the canonisation of Webster, there is little doubt that the nineteenth century witnessed a shift in the reputation of Webster (along with, it must be said, a number of other Elizabethan and Jacobean dramatists) from an obscure figure to a writer at the heart of literary and critical debate. The key figure in this debate is undoubtedly the essayist Charles Lamb (1775–1834), whose *Specimens of English Dramatic Poets who Lived about the time of Shakespeare* (1808) reprinted selections from the Elizabethan and Jacobean dramatists (not widely available to nineteenth-century readers), and had high praise for Webster. Initial reactions to Lamb's valorisation of Webster were mixed, but as the century moved forwards, his opinions came to carry more and more weight, continuing to shape critical discussion of Webster's plays even after the dramatist had been more or less accepted into the canon. Another influential essayist, William Hazlitt (1778–1830), continued Lamb's high estimation of Webster, suggesting in 1821 that his two tragedies 'come the nearest to Shakespear[e] of any things we have upon record' (Hazlitt 1821: 124). For those throughout the century who wished to promote the claims of Webster, this sense that he was second only to Shakespeare as an English tragedian of emotional intensity was often repeated. The influence of Lamb, keenly felt by Hazlitt, was no doubt also an impetus towards the first collected edition of Webster's work, edited by Alexander Dyce

(1798–1869), and published in 1830. Again, Webster was not alone among the Renaissance dramatists in receiving such attention; but Dyce was typical in finding *The White Devil* 'a play of extraordinary power' (Dyce 1930: vii). Later critics concurred, the American essayist Edwin P. Whittle writing in 1869 that 'of all the contemporaries of Shakespeare, Webster is the most Shakespearian' (Moore 1981: 104), and the literary historian George Saintsbury arguing in 1887 that '*The White Devil* remains one of the most glorious works of the period' (Saintsbury 1911: 275).

Unanimity of critical opinion is rare in the history of Webster scholarship, however, and there were a number of critics with little good to say for the dramatist; more interestingly, perhaps, even among those critics interested in Webster, there remained a significant amount of disagreement as to which aspects of the work showed artistic achievement, and which were to be considered deficient. Gradually over the course of the century, this led to a split between the 'dramatic' Webster (often considered lacking) and the 'poetic' Webster (often considered as a brilliant writer), a division of duty which Webster himself may have recognised (although the dramatic conventions by which the nineteenth-century critics judged him would have been alien to an early modern dramatist). As early as 1818, in *Blackwood's Edinburgh Magazine*, charges of poor dramatic workmanship were being laid at the feet of Webster, 'Christoper North' complaining that *The White Devil* 'is so disjointed in its action [. . .] and there is, throughout, such a mixture of the horrible and the absurd – the comic and the tragic – the pathetic and the ludicrous' (Moore 1981: 56). This anonymous critic correctly identified the aesthetic relativism which this book argues is one of Webster's dramatic achievements – but it clearly was not perceived as an achievement by 'North'. Such criticisms were widely felt in the nineteenth century, as a number of critics lambasted Webster's highly distinctive dramaturgy; another anonymous critic, writing in 1833, considered that 'the judicious formation of his plots and arrangement of incidents do not seem to have been much studied by him' (Moore 1981: 77). Even Webster's champions sometimes repeated this view when they spoke of the 'passages of exquisite poetic beauty' 'scattered throughout the play' (Dyce 1830: ix), the 'flashes of genius' (Moore 1981: 59), and the 'wonderful flashes of poetry' (Saintsbury 1911: 276): all of which contribute, whether intentionally or not, to a view of Webster as a writer of great poetry rather than of great drama.

Equally conflicted, and subject to change over the course of the century, was the moral response appropriate to *The White Devil*, a subject of significant concern not so much to the Romantics of the earlier part of the century, but certainly to their Victorian successors. Whereas Webster's interest in sin, sex, and death could be viewed as a proto-'gothicism', anticipating the Romantic vogue for the gothic, it could also be interpreted as an index of immoral depravity. Hazlitt, for example, though less easily offended than some of his contemporaries, nevertheless felt that Webster could carry 'terror and pity to a [. . .] painful and *sometimes unwarrantable* excess' (Hazlitt 1821: 124; emphasis mine). The anonymous critic of 1833, meanwhile, characterised Webster as a ghoulish grave-lurker, in a portrait which continues to influence some readings of the drama:

> He loves to dwell [. . .] among scutcheons, and hourglasses, and coffins, and all the painful emblems of mortality; an epitaph to him is a joke, and a sexton is his bedfellow and friend. He has a dagger more often in his hand than a knife, and he carries a phial of poison in his pocket [. . .] His genius, like the yew-tree which he describes, flourishes best where its roots are in the tomb. (Moore 1981: 77)

Such sentiments were not universal but they were certainly widely felt. Nowhere were they more forcefully, and moralistically, propounded, than in the work of Charles Kingsley, who thought *The White Devil* a 'story [. . .] of sin and horror [. . .] made up of the fiercest and basest passions' (Kingsley 1873: 15). For Kingsley, 'the study of human nature is not Webster's aim. He has to arouse terror and pity, *not thought*, and he does it *in his own way*, by blood and fury, madmen and screech-owls' (Kingsley 1873: 15; my emphasis); here the critic displays an interest in the internal workings of Webster's mind, something which would be developed in later criticism.

The Early Twentieth Century: The Horrors of War

The twentieth century, of course, witnessed the professionalisation of literary criticism, as the practice became firmly established as a mode of academic enquiry. The nineteenth-century debates around Webster meant that his work was well-placed to be drawn into the emerging canon. Perhaps more importantly, however, the horrors of the Great War (and, later, the Second World War) suggested to many that Webster may have had more insight into the corruption and depravity of human nature than the earlier gentleman-critics could have realised. It was in 1919, just one year after the end of the most horrific conflict that Europe had yet witnessed, that T. S. Eliot memorably suggested that:

> Webster was much possessed by death
> And saw the skull beneath the skin;
> And breastless creatures under ground
> Leaned backward with a lipless grin.
>
> Daffodil bulbs instead of balls
> Stared from the sockets of the eyes!
> He knew that thought clings round dead limbs
> Tightening its lusts and luxuries. (Eliot 1974: 55–6)

If Eliot, writing at the close of one period of barbarity, was compelled to draw on Webster, it may be significant that in 1939, as the world was sliding towards an even more destructive war, the critic James Smith saw Webster not so much as 'possessed by death', as engaged in 'the portrayal of a world of evil' (Smith 1969: 131). For Smith, this is the dramatic aim of *The White Devil*; and the way in which Webster achieves this aim stands as a response to those detractors who claim that he 'lacks constructive ability' (Smith 1969: 116). Hence, the unconventional dramatic construction of *The White Devil*: sentences, speeches, scenes, even whole acts, 'seem not so much to follow and resume, as to qualify or comment on one another as they lie side by side' (Smith 1969: 118). This is an important insight, and accords with the Websterian practice of dramatic construction by units or 'blocks'. This may have developed from his experience as a collaborative craftsman in the early part of his theatrical career, and certainly is significant for an appreciation of the relativist approach to aesthetic value on display. For Smith, the acknowledgement of this has a significant impact on the way in which an audience engages with the play: 'the spectator is required to judge not so much between statements, as to base a judgement upon a group of them' (Smith 1969: 119). The dramatic writing, then, 'almost ceases to be writing and to be dramatic; it becomes operatic and almost a score' (Smith 1969: 126). As the play progresses, 'the scenes interpenetrate one another, are to be thought of, so to speak, as existing side by side' (Smith 1969: 129). The scenes and acts 'show different aspects of the same theme – the workings of evil' (Smith 1969: 130). The corollary of this method of construction means that those nineteenth-century critics who praised the play's characterisation of Vittoria were, in effect, misled; or at least, had focused their energies in the wrong location: 'there is no character in *The White Devil* – neither Vittoria nor Flamineo nor Cornelia – through which the play can be looked at' (Smith 1969: 130). *The White Devil* thus differs from most Renaissance plays, not because of its interest in 'evil', but because 'the evil world is presented from within' (Smith 1969: 132).

Similarly, David Cecil, writing in 1949, imagined Webster's 'tragic vision' as that of a 'fallen place', where 'all activities are tainted with sin' and where 'evil is the controlling force' (Cecil 1969: 150). Although 'in Webster's view people commit crimes [. . .] because they are corrupted by that original sin with which all mortal flesh is tainted', nevertheless Webster's primary interest, for Cecil, lies in 'the intellectual sinner' (Cecil 1969: 151). Cecil's vocabulary is not unlike that of some of Webster's nineteenth-century detractors: he writes of Webster's 'horrors [. . .] ghosts and tortures [. . .] spiritual terror [. . .] the grotesque and the horrible' (Cecil 1969: 155–7). Yet he praises Webster as a dramatist able to expose the 'fundamental hollowness' of the world (Cecil 1969: 155). By way of contrast, Ian Jack, writing in the same year in the influential journal *Scrutiny*, castigated Webster as a 'decadent' with 'no deeper purpose than to make our flesh creep' (Jack 1969: 164). For Jack, Webster singularly fails to achieve 'a profound *and balanced* insight into life' and hence is incapable of writing 'great tragedy' (Jack 1969: 158). Webster is guilty of 'artistic insincerity', 'an outlook of life as narrow as it is intense', and, finally, of being 'a trifle ridiculous' (Jack 1969: 162–4). Jack's outlook is typical of the journal in which his work appeared; *Scrutiny* was heavily influenced by its most significant contributor and editor, F. R. Leavis. For Leavis, the great works of English literature were to be understood as cornerstones of civilisation, accessible only to an educated and discriminating minority, and opposed to the 'mass culture' made available by industrial processes and technological advances (the cinema, for example). Given the populist and sensationalist streak in Webster's drama, it is unsurprising that *Scrutiny* would be hostile to the dramatist. Indeed, Webster's aesthetic relativism displays a view of literature completely at odds with the Leavisite project. Thus the nineteenth-century debate continued even into the middle years of the twentieth century.

The Later Twentieth Century: Political Criticism

As the century wore on, critics were generally more inclined to take the side of Cecil, although many shared a portion of Jack's cynicism for Webster's dramatic strategies; increasingly, then, a more subtle and nuanced vision of the dramatist emerged. Neither simply a great tragedian, nor a purveyor of cheap thrills, Webster came increasingly to be seen as a playwright whose work troubled the very distinction between the two categories. Hereward T. Price argued in 1955 that 'in Webster no one is thoroughly evil'; the 'love' of Brachiano and Vittoria, although 'a source of so much evil and suffering', nevertheless remains 'a thing of strength and beauty' (Price 1969: 190). Thus simplistic visions of Webster's art and morality were to be eschewed: 'strip some veils of appearance from them [that is, the central characters] and they are foul; strip those other veils from them and their hearts are seen to harbour an inviolable greatness' (Price 1969: 191).

Such conflicts between critics make the job of determining a consensus opinion on Webster very difficult. John Russell Brown, editing the play in 1960, was forced to concede that 'critical opinion cannot speak with certain or united voice about Webster's purposes' (Brown 1969: 240). The task of an editor, of course, is different to the task of an individual critic, and always involves synthesising different viewpoints; but clearly, Webster was still causing significant critical disagreement at this point. But the view which Brown outlines of Webster as 'a man halting between his inherited and his individual values' was, perhaps, growing in significance (Brown 1969: 240); this is Webster as transitional figure, as the poet of the emerging modern 'individual' striving to survive in a corrupt world. For G. K. Hunter, writing in the same year as Brown, Webster's Italy is 'a symbolic world where the individual is lost in the mazes of political activity', a world of 'competing individualisms' where 'the individuals are too isolated from each other ever to make a community of purpose' (Hunter 1969: 262). In 1970, A. J. Smith had similar to things to say, albeit with slightly more cynicism than the earlier critics:

> This is hardly a play in which a hero elects to press through with things to the end on some principle or driving design. What it shows us instead are characters moving by emergent expedients to self-regarding ends, whose tragedy lies just in their inevitable collisions with the emergent wills of others. (Smith 1970: 82)

Such readings all hint at a move towards analysing Webster's play in terms of its representation of a particular political culture, and of the stresses of the relationships between individuals and wider social pressures in such circumstances; as we shall see below, such a way of reading the play became increasingly common in succeeding decades.

Yet these 'political' readings of the play were not yet totally dominant in Webster criticism; for example, Ralph Berry's *The Art of John Webster* (1972), still one of the most significant books yet published on the dramatist, remains concerned with the abstract philosophical tenor of Webster's play:

> I am ready to see Webster's religious allusions as an extension of his sensationalism. The horror of the hereafter complements the physical horror of the stage. Such a reading is confirmed, for me, by the consideration that Webster's philosophical and

psychological concerns seem largely unrelated to the central Calvinist issues [. . .] So the status of evil in *The White Devil* remains on the level of metaphor. The metaphors are varied, powerful, suggestive. But they lack, and are meant to lack, theological precision and commitment. (Berry 1972: 98)

Increasingly, though, critical attention moved towards the social and the political; for M. C. Bradbrook, writing in 1980, Webster's distinctive formal technique of highlighting perspectival differences in appearance (one, although not the only, aspect of his aesthetic relativism) had a social significance as well as a purely dramatic function:

> Webster's relating of these two levels, so that a character is seen or sees himself first in one relation and then in another, means that, with his tragic pattern, he works in the social developments of family structure as he saw it evolving around him, with the competitive struggle of the underling who must acquire some hold over his lord if he is to feel secure. (Bradbrook 1980: 128)

So the disorientation-effect of Websterian drama is significant, and not a result of clumsy construction, as earlier critics had argued; similarly, Jacqueline Pearson, writing in the same year as Bradbrook, emphasises the 'ambiguities and images of relativity' in *The White Devil* (Pearson 1980: 83), and thus comes the closest of any critic to pinpointing aesthetic relativism as the driving force behind the play's construction. For Pearson, 'Webster has strong reservations about the ability of any simple genre to depict the complex world' (Pearson 1980: 83). Thus, what had been seen by an earlier generation as an illustration of Webster's lack of skill as a dramatist was increasingly coming to be seen as an integral part of his social and aesthetic vision.

RECENT READINGS

Recent critical readings of *The White Devil* have continued this focus on the structural and technical aspects of Webster's play, but have also widened the horizons of Webster commentary, by exploring the ways in which the play engages with wider cultural concerns, including race and gender. The following section will identify some of the key preoccupations in recent criticism of *The White Devil*, beginning by examining the 'technical' concerns of current critics, before moving on to the wider 'cultural' concerns.

Genre

Despite the intense discussions of Webster's dramatic strategies which took place over the course of the nineteenth and twentieth centuries, there remains a sense in which the dramaturgy of *The White Devil* – its aesthetic relativism – remains challenging and, as mentioned in the previous section, disorientating for an audience. Critics are still unable to exactly identify what genre of drama the play most clearly fits into: there is widespread agreement that it is a tragedy, but beyond that there is little consensus. Many critics argue that it is a 'revenge tragedy', a type of drama which came in and out of fashion in the English Renaissance; the two most famous examples, Kyd's *Spanish Tragedy* and Shakespeare's *Hamlet*, were both composed some time before Webster's play. But – in addition to its explicit borrowings from Shakespeare's *Hamlet* – *The White Devil* is structurally much more complicated than either of those plays; the clarity of a clearly defined revenger, exacting revenge on a clearly defined opponent, is simply not present in Webster's play, which offers a series of revenges, and little sense of a clearly defined avenging hero with whom the audience can identify. Some critics, then, prefer to speak of the 'elements of revenge tragedy' present in the play, rather than fully identifying the play with that genre (Williamson 2007: 485).

Nevertheless, both critics and directors remain somewhat 'non-plussed', in the terminology used by the play's most recent editor (Webster 1995: 57). For this critic, recent readings and productions of the play have suggested 'an uncertainty as to how the play might convincingly be presented in other than sensational terms' (Webster 1995: 57). However, there are some strategies which have been used by those who want to demonstrate the play's anti-sensationalism (or at least to suggest that the play is not just a sensationalist 'shocker'). For instance, recent readings by both Martin Wiggins and Judith Weil have suggested the extent to which Webster draws on classical influences in this play. Of course, the culture of the ancient world was a vital resource for all writers working in the 'Renaissance' period, but it is an aspect of Webster's art which has frequently been overlooked, perhaps because it sits uneasily with a reductive view of the dramatist as purveyor of cheap theatrical thrills. Wiggins emphasises the important influence of a second-hand classicism, Ben Jonson's Roman tragedy *Sejanus*; for Wiggins, Webster's famous trial scene in this play is based on that of Jonson, while even the typography of the printed edition of *The White Devil* is influenced by the Quarto of *Sejanus* (Wiggins 1997: 469). For Weil, meanwhile, the importance of classical culture in Webster's play is highlighted by his intertextual allusions to 'the potent figures of Juno and Hecuba' (Weil 1999: 329). Weil argues that Isabella and Cornelia are ambiguously linked in Webster's rhetoric to the classical figures, and thus that 'their suffering bespeaks a genuine attachment to those they love' (Weil 1999: 336). At the same time, however, early modern theatrical culture was such that the influence of the classics could quite easily be tied to popular images of spectacular violence; both Kyd's *Spanish Tragedy* and Shakespeare's *Titus Andronicus* are examples of how this could be represented on the tragic stage. Webster's dramatic experiments in this play still appear to be quite distinct from those earlier dramas.

These questions of the generic status of the play have been matched by a continuing exploration of the more broadly technical aspects of Webster's craft and, perhaps surprisingly, a continued interest in the moral schema of Webster's imagined world. In terms of the latter, David Gunby discusses the 'orthodox moral views' conveyed by Webster's frequent use of *sententiae* (Webster 1995: 60), although he is well aware that 'for many the sententiae are singularly unconvincing' (Webster 1995: 60). More intriguingly, Gunby goes on to make claims for the moral significance of the play's overall structure. Rejecting the claims of earlier critics that the play is structured either as a series of fragments or as an artless aggregation, Gunby claims that *The White Devil* is 'a carefully wrought and highly intricate artefact' (Webster 1995: 61).

Many current critics (myself included) would agree with this statement, although there may well be less consensus with the claim which Gunby builds onto this formal judgment: 'the play possesses both a subtle and highly integrated structure and (embodied in that structure) a moral schema' (Webster 1995: 61). Many critics, finding the moral structures of early modern England significantly in tension with their own ethical assumptions, have been reluctant to engage with the question of 'morality' or 'evil', though it does seem to have been an issue with which Webster's original audiences may have engaged.

For Gunby, then, 'the play works cyclically, by exploiting repetition, parallelism, and analogy in language, character, and incident' (Webster 1995: 61). Webster uses a number of characteristic formal strategies, including 'the integration of language and action in one expressive figure' and 'a pairing or doubling of characters and situations' (for example, Lodovico and Flamineo are both malcontents, Monticelso and Francisco both revengers; Webster 1995: 61). Thus, this 'complex system of patterning [. . .] connects apparently disparate and unrelated elements' (Webster 1995: 78). The effect of this structure, for Gunby, is to encourage an audience to make moral interpretations of the action presented to them: the play demonstrates a 'causal relationship between crime and punishment – a retributive pattern' (Webster 1995: 78). Following this argument allows Gunby to suggest that Francisco's apparent escape from punishment at the play's end is, in fact, not an escape, but simply a temporary reprieve: 'we can be left both with an awareness of the continuing presence of evil in the world and [. . .] with the sense of a moral order which contains and eventually destroys the evildoer' (Webster 1995: 80). As this chapter suggests, the idea that *The White Devil* contains an identifiable 'moral order' is one which many readers and audiences find challenging; but Gunby's wider points about the structure and dramatic technique of the play are useful and convincing, and can be seen to support this book's contention that Webster should be seen as an aesthetic relativist (though not necessarily a moral relativist).

If Gunby's reading focuses on the distinctly formal qualities of the play's structure, that of Wiggins is more clearly interested in the formal structures of the play *in performance*, particularly in the way in which Webster constructs his scenes with a careful attention to the number of bodies present on stage at any one time. Wiggins's argument is primarily directed at textual editors of the play, who have tended to excise so-called 'ghost' characters from the early printed editions when editing them for modern readers. A 'ghost' character is one who is marked as present on stage, but given no lines to speak: many editors consider the inclusion of these characters to be an oversight on the part of the writer or printer, and so remove them from modern stage directions; but, as Wiggins argues, 'characters may be eloquent merely by their silent presence on stage' (Wiggins 1997: 453); thus, 'we can no longer assume that Cariola, or any other figure in Webster, should not be present simply because she has nothing to say' (Wiggins 1997: 453). This straightforward point is used to highlight a significant feature of Webster's stagecraft: the 'densely-populated' nature of the stage, including 'six leading roles' (Wiggins 1997: 457). Moreover, the play 'flouts the common-sense principles governing the size of the cast' and frequently introduces characters who are 'surplus to requirements' (Wiggins 1997: 458).

Wiggins identifies two main reasons for the large number of parts in this play: the first is to create atmosphere and a sense of place, to convey 'the populousness and complexity of the metropolis' (Wiggins 1997: 459). More broadly speaking, furthermore, 'the simple physical fact of the number of bodies present, whether speaking or silent, can influence our perception of a moment' (Wiggins 1997: 461). Thus Webster can use the bodies of actors as shorthand to quickly demonstrate the relative intimacy or publicness of a particular scene; as Wiggins indicates, the stage is 'fullest at the start of the trial scene . . . there are at least nineteen [actors] present' (Wiggins 1997: 461). In contrast, 'the numbers dwindle to four for the moment when the little Giovanni brings his uncle news of Isabella's death' (Wiggins 1997: 461). Thus the bodies of the actors are used by Webster as part of the same intricate structure of paralleling, repetition, and cyclicity which Gunby identifies as central to the dramatic strategies of this play.

Implicit in Wiggins' reading of *The White Devil* is a sense that the physical impact of the play on a theatre audience is very different to the experience of a reader of the text, whether in the seventeenth century or today. Other critics have been more explicit in identifying the text's conception of its audience as an appropriate and necessary area for criticism to explore. Gunby's reading of the trial scene, for example, suggests that Vittoria's plea for the trial to take place in English rather than in Latin works to include the audience in the Red Bull theatre in the action, as many of the audience members at this particular venue would not have possessed the educational background necessary to understand spoken Latin (Webster 1995: 72). Indeed, Gunby emphasises how Vittoria not infrequently works to bring the audience onto her side in the course of the play, a technique which makes a complex emotional and moral engagement with the play more likely. When Vittoria addresses the Ambassadors in the trial scene, for instance, Gunby suggests that she 'may easily include the audience in a wider sweep of her arm, for here, as in so much that she says and does in this scene, she actively solicits our support' (Webster 1995: 73). Similarly, the action on stage frequently presents the Ambassadors as observers, suggesting that they are related in quite specific ways to the audience. Significantly for a London audience, it is particularly 'the English Ambassador's comments, to which, in their acuity and balance, we might be expected to subscribe' (Webster 1995: 80). Thus the play is intensely aware of the audience witnessing the performance, and frequently works to engage that audience deeply with the action presented on stage.

More recently, Katherine M. Carey has suggested that Webster's ways of engaging the theatrical audience in this play are broadly similar to what current theorists of media and spectacle call 'hypermediacy' (Carey 2007: 73). Carey suggests that 'hypermediacy expresses itself as multiplicity which makes multiple acts of representation visible' (Carey 2007: 73), and that this is particularly relevant to Webster's use of the Renaissance convention of the 'dumb show':

> The Renaissance dumb show within a text is a performed play within a play in which audience members watch the play within a frame; then, within that frame, they witness yet another play. The dumb show by its very nature builds layers of hypermediation into the performance. (Carey 2007: 74)

The effect of this, Carey claims, is quite different to the audience's emotional engagement with Vittoria which Gunby sees as a feature of the trial scene; rather than engagement at this point, the audience experiences detachment, the dumb show 'serving as a very present reminder that the play is just a play' (Carey 2007: 74). Thus Webster – in keeping with his refusal to privilege one form over another – uses a number of different techniques to effect audience engagement or detachment depending on the specific theatrical effect desired at the particular point of the play.

In keeping with recent critical emphases on the materiality of Renaissance play-texts (that is, on reading the original printed documents as texts in themselves, with all their apparent inconsistencies and irregularities) and on the instability of such texts (that is, the growing recognition that printed texts of plays in the early modern period represent not a definitive version of the play, but perhaps just one version among many), examinations of the textual history of *The White Devil* have also begun recently to appear. The first printed text of *The White Devil*, however, is different from many printed play-texts of the period, in that we know the playwright was personally involved in the publication of the text. Often, in the period, playwrights relinquished control over their scripts once they had been given to the theatre companies, much as any other producer of a craft or commodity doesn't claim ownership of an object after it has been sold: the theatre company may then decide to print the text, although not normally when the play is still popular on stage. As suggested at the start of this chapter, though, *The White Devil* was a commercial failure on its first performance, and Webster seems to have instigated the printing of the text himself.

The text thus has a significantly higher level of 'authority' than most Renaissance play-texts, at least as far as such authority can be located in the figure of the playwright (for a more detailed examination of early modern concepts of 'authorship' and 'authority', see pp. 19–20). It is therefore not typical of early modern play-texts. Nevertheless, many of the concerns which editors have about other early printed texts can also be applied to first editions of *The White Devil*, printed in a format known as Quarto (about the size of a modern paperback, and relatively inexpensive, this was the most common format for individual play-texts in the period). As discussed above, Wiggins has examined the presence of potential 'ghost' characters in the Quarto editions of this play, concluding that 'the Quarto text introduces these characters to the reader in a confusing and unsatisfactory way' (Wiggins 1997: 449). Suggesting that textual anomalies were apparent even to later seventeenth-century readers and printers, Wiggins suggests that the uneasy relationship between text and performance is a feature of the early editions of *The White Devil*, as it is for other Renaissance play-texts:

> If an editor allows equal weight to the alternative theoretical possibility that they may have been retained in performance, and considers each of the four [individual instances of possible 'ghosts'] in terms of the individual problems and opportunities which that possibility might entail, then different textual options will become available in each case. (Wiggins 1997: 453)

So a number of what this chapter has called 'technical' issues are still the subject of critical discussion in Webster studies: while many critics now agree with Gunby that there is significance and meaning in the play's structure, not all would readily accept the proposition that structure carries a moral significance; the exact generic classification of the play still eludes critics; the relationship which the text imagines with its audience has been elucidated, yet still remains complex and perhaps underexplored; and the possibility of achieving a 'definitive' text of any Renaissance play is increasingly coming to be seen as an impossible goal. But if the 'technical' aspects of the play continue to cause some disagreement among critics, such agreements are perhaps overshadowed by the fierce debates surrounding the 'cultural' aspects of the play.

Gender and Culture

The treatment of religion – Catholicism in particular – is a case in point. Despite the presence of an intensely-realised Catholic community in both of Webster's major works, the representation of religion in *The White Devil* was for many years not at the forefront of critical attention, largely because it was assumed that Webster was simply partaking of a crude and reductive anti-Catholicism prevalent in seventeenth-century Protestant London. However, recent work by historians has demonstrated that the English Reformation was a much lengthier and less immediately popular movement than had hitherto been assumed. Literary critics are increasingly alert, therefore, to the complexities of the representation of Catholicism in English Renaissance drama, as a hostile anti-Catholicism – while undoubtedly present in early modern England – was far from the only imaginative response to the religion available.

In staging Catholicism, then, Webster stages a religion which still had some followers in England, even if they were unable to admit to their faith publicly; perhaps more importantly, he stages a religion which had been officially sanctioned until only a few generations previously. In a recent reading of the play, for example, Elizabeth Williamson has pointed out how one of the most overtly 'Catholic' of stage properties used in the play – Cornelia's crucifix – functions in the play not simply as an emblem of Catholic difference from the Protestant audience, but rather 'as the embodiment of family unity' (Williamson 2007: 473); thus, she claims, the play 'reinforces a point made elsewhere by historians of the Reformation: namely, that in many cases Catholic objects survived by being translated into new contexts' (Williamson 2007: 473). If the play's audience may have seen the crucifix primarily as a family heirloom rather than as a marker of religious identity, then this must lead critics to consider how other aspects of Catholicism would have been interpreted by an early modern English audience. (However, see pp. 47–55, where I argue that the Catholicism of the crucifix *is* significant for an interpretation of the play.)

As Williamson points out, crucifixes were used as family heirlooms in early modern England, albeit primarily in families who maintained a secret Catholic faith, known as 'recusants' (Williamson 2007: 475); by drawing on this aspect of Catholic domestic life, *The White Devil* can perhaps be seen to 'promote a more compassionate view of Catholic practice by pointing to the interpenetration of religious rituals and social traditions' (Williamson 2007: 479). The conventional view of the play as promoting a popular anti-Catholicism, then, is incorrect; or rather, it is *partly* incorrect, as this play which structurally depends on the juxtaposition of opposing and potentially incoherent points of view, adopts a similar strategy in its representation of Catholic practice: *The White Devil* thus 'anticipates the complex perspectives on religion offered in Webster's subsequent tragedies' (Williamson 2007: 486). Such a view, it should also be noted, offers support to those critics who wish to argue that the play presents a complex intellectual and emotional experience to its audience, rather than mere sensationalism.

If religion represents a cultural preoccupation of early modern England which is only now beginning to be fully explored by critics, the study of gender, and particularly the representation of women in male-authored texts, has a much longer critical history. From the earliest stages of Webster's critical afterlife, it was generally recognised that his two major plays were atypical in placing a woman at the centre of the play, and in having the central female character also the title character. With the rise of critical feminism in the twentieth century, the nature of Webster's women has occasioned much commentary and debate. It seems worth noting that Vittoria is the central character of *The White Devil* in an unconventional way; of course, as noted above, this is a play with a series of leading characters, rather than a star performer at the centre. Indeed, the theatrical conventions of the early modern stage make it very difficult for dramatists to write plays with women at their centre, as female characters were played by boys. As the boys were junior members of the companies, and a company's leading actor would always have been an adult male (at least if it was an adult company, such as Webster's major plays were composed for), then it would be practically impossible for a female character to dominate a play in the way that Marlowe's or Shakespeare's male protagonists do. Nevertheless, the cultural and practical forces working against a female character at the centre of a play make it particularly interesting that Webster chose to pursue this strategy not once, but twice.

Vittoria, despite her charisma and magnetism, remains potentially problematic for a modern feminist audience. Gunby rightly claims that:

> She is all the more problematic because of the way in which Webster presents her – she is never alone on stage, for

instance, and never soliloquizes. Moreover, Webster severely limits her stage appearances, offering different facets of her personality each time she does appear. In I.ii we see the bored wife (and also the frightened daughter), in III.ii the defiant and resourceful woman, in IV.i the outraged mistress, in V.iii (briefly) the grief-stricken wife, and in V.vi the courageous tragic heroine. Webster seems, in fact, to be working in a fashion quite consciously disjunctive in his presentation of Vittoria. (Webster 1995: 59)

Each of these points requires some critical attention. The fact that Vittoria never soliloquises means that an audience is never privy to her inmost thoughts and motivations; that she cannot enter into an alliance with the audience, in the way that a villain like Richard III or Iago can; and that the play partakes of a discourse which resists granting full subjectivity (the experience of one's own self-consciousness) to women (on subjectivity, see p. 123). The fact that she is presented in a number of stereotypically female roles means that she is always a convention of a male-authored narrative; Gunby's sense that this is a deliberate strategy on Webster's part may be correct, but it would not be difficult to construct a feminist reading of the play which castigates this strategy of representing women as one of a series of social types.

Vittoria is undoubtedly at the centre of the play, and audiences are frequently drawn to her, perhaps because of the enigmatic qualities which many critics claim for her; but she is by no means the only female character in the play, and a critic interested in the representation of women in the play must be prepared to look a little further than just Vittoria. As mentioned earlier, Weil is particularly interested in the 'old wives' of the play (Weil 1999: 328), suggesting that Cornelia and Isabella 'can shock an audience' and 'have an extraordinary effectiveness,' just as Vittoria can (Weil 1999: 331). While Webster may draw on some of the gendered stereotypes of his era, presenting women as 'burdened with overwhelming and contradictory emotions,' Weil suggests that his allusions to other texts which represent emotionally-burdened women, 'presuppose[s] his scrutiny of the contexts from which he derives them' (Weil 1999: 333) and thus, presumably, that again the play reveals a considerable level of complexity in its treatment of contemporary cultural concerns.

The question of gender is intimately related to two other issues which inform much contemporary discussion of the play: the question of national identity and the question of racial difference. In terms of the first of these closely related concerns, Lara Bovilsky has recently argued for the significance of English Italianate drama (including *The White Devil*) in contributing to an ongoing discussion about the nature of English identity in the early seventeenth century: 'English Italianate dramas,' she claims, 'effectively testified to and promoted experiences of diversity and alterity within the imagination of the English subject' (Bovilsky 2003: 626). But questions of national difference are also linked to questions of gender and racial difference, albeit in complex ways:

> English standards of female beauty not only derive from, but are no less disturbing than dark, Italian ones, for they require frequent and fluid demonstrations of shame and shock, blood marking feminine (im)modesty. But blushing and blanching are something of a problem, for in this nexus, sudden blushing indicates that seeming fair skin may always transform into (or already conceals) darkness, and sudden paleness implies that skin was never as light as it might have been. (Bovilsky 2003: 643)

If the difference between dark and light skin, then, cannot be taken for granted, neither perhaps can the difference between man and woman, or the difference between English and Italian. *The White Devil*, certainly, aims to display its Italians as exotic, the better to give its English audience a sense of what distinguishes them from the foreign bodies on stage (it is notable, of course, that Webster gives significant lines to the English Ambassador). But this too, is complicated, as English Renaissance literary culture is heavily indebted to the cultural example of Italy, particularly (as Bovilsky points out) in terms of Italian Petrarchan poetics, and its hugely significant impact on English Renaissance literature. Very little of the poetry of the English Renaissance could have been composed without the influence of Petrarch and the Petrarchans, and thus the attempt to present Italy as different, as non-English, in the drama of the period is always riven with a potential tension.

If concepts of gendered and national difference are both pro-moted and interrogated by *The White Devil*, then, it may come as no surprise that the play also reveals an interest in racial differ-ence, drawing not just on the assumed differences of complexion between the English and the Italians, but also staging a number of Moorish characters, one of whom is female (hence played by an English boy), one of whom doesn't speak, and has been identi-fied as a 'ghost' by some editors, and one of whom is Francisco in disguise (an Englishman, disguised as an Italian, disguised as a Moor, and, of course, using the same theatrical make-up as the 'real' Moors in the play). The discourses of race in the play – and the ways in which they intersect with the discourses of gender and of nation – function in a number of different ways, as recent critics have shown. Wiggins, for example, outlines how the play's title demands to be read, not just in gendered, but also in racial-ised terms: the play 'involves a pair of devils – the white (Vittoria) being coupled with the black in Zanche [devils were convention-ally presented as black in early modern England], demonstrating the Elizabethan proverb that the white devil is more dangerous than the black' (Wiggins 1997: 470). Furthermore, black and white at times function as a simplistic moral index in this play where moral conventions are generally extremely complicated and dif-ficult to follow: 'Francisco exemplifies the moral degeneration which his now-blackened features symbolise' (Wiggins 1997: 470). Wiggins also argues that Jaques (identified as a Moor, of course, in Webster's stage direction) is not a 'ghost' character, but would have been witnessed on stage, thus 'contribut[ing] in a small way to the exotic, Mediterranean flavour of the play's setting, as well as pointing up the title's ironic manipulation of the symbolic values of black and white' (Wiggins 1997: 455).

That the representation of such racial 'others' is an intrinsic part of the play's strategy of exploring the nature of national identity is strongly argued by Bovilsky: 'early modern English vocabular-ies of national and racial difference share terminology, trading on imagery of moral and physical blackness or alien subjectivity, and exhibiting a heightened concern with questions of blood and its purity' (Bovilsky 2003: 628). Thus the Moorish characters are identified with Italy (and, one might suppose, Islam is associated with Catholicism), as instances of non-English exoticism. As Bovilsky argues, Italianate drama frequently stages not just Italians, but also 'Jews, Moors, and Turks,' all of whom would have been perceived as 'racialized' by an English audience (Bovilsky 2003: 637). What one finds in *The White Devil*, therefore, is 'a dense combination of dis- and crossidentification, English and Italian, nation and race' (Bovilsky 2003: 637). But if these strategies of identification can never be absolute, aligning them with gendered difference – that is, with woman as different from the assumed normative of man – creates a figure with whom the audience finds it much more difficult to empathise. This, according to Bovilsky, is the reason why the female Moor Zanche is treated in the way she is:

> the character Zanche would seem to stand apart as figured in unequivocal blackness, exempt from the ambiguously positive connotations of white devilry. A rare female Moorish character, she is the object of casual scorn or violent loathing from virtually all the characters (Vittoria excepted), which is often shocking in the specificity of its racism. (Bovilsky 2003: 645)

Thus it is the 'black devil' – the female, Moorish servant – who is most fully demonised in the play; Zanche is not afforded either the charisma or the eloquence of the titular 'White Devil'.

In tandem, then, with continuing explorations of the original and (some might say) idiosyncratic dramatic technique employed by Webster in this play, critics in recent decades have been acutely aware of how *The White Devil* is acutely preoccupied with cultural issues central to early modernity: the role of religion (especially Catholicism) in post-Reformation England and, more broadly, Europe; the nature of gender difference, and the roles and opportunities to be afforded to men and women in society; the nature of national identity, and the relationship between Italy and England; and the nature of racial difference. All of these concerns, it should be said, are affected by the unique structure of *The White Devil*; many of them appear again in Webster's next play, but the manner in which they are presented to the audience is rather different. *The White Devil* and *The Duchess of Malfi* share many of the same concerns; but, despite the aesthetic relativism underlying Webster's career, dramatically speaking, they are radically different theatrical experiences.

CHAPTER 4

'Rich Tissue': *The Duchess of Malfi*

SUMMARY AND ANALYSIS

Raising a Monument

The prefatory material to the first edition of *The Duchess of Malfi* (1623) has a rather different tone to that of *The White Devil* (1612). Whereas the earlier play displayed the voice of an author eager to defend his work against a hostile audience reaction, the *Duchess*'s prefatory materials are lavish in their praise of this 'masterpiece' (Commendatory Verses, 34). The play was first performed in 1614, and was a huge success. The difference in reception of Webster's two tragedies can be gauged by the timespan between initial performance and publication: for *The White Devil* less than a year, for *The Duchess of Malfi* some nine years – a good indication that the King's Men considered the latter a valuable playing text.

The prefatory material consists of two parts: Webster's dedication of his play to 'George Harding, Baron Berkeley of Berkeley Castle' (Dedication, 1–2), and a series of 'Commendatory Verses' in praise of the play, written by Webster's fellow-playwrights Thomas Middleton, William Rowley, and John Ford. Both the dedication and the verses consciously echo one of the central preoccupations of the play: how to construct a legacy of honour in a world dominated by cruelty and horror. For both Webster and the other playwrights, the answer lies, perhaps unsurprisingly, in the power of art. Webster tries to persuade his dedicatee of the posthumous benefits of serving as a patron to poets while alive:

> poets have kissed the hands of great princes and drawn their gentle eyes to look down upon their sheets of paper when the poets themselves were bound up in their winding sheets. The like courtesy from your lordship shall make you live in your grave and laurel spring out of it. (Dedication, 19–23)

The dedicatory verses, meanwhile, shift the focus to Webster, claiming that his play will serve as a fitting memorial: 'thou by this work of fame / Hast well provided for thy living name'; 'Thy monument is raised in thy lifetime'; 'thy epitaph, only the title be – / Write *Duchess*, that will fetch a tear for thee'; '[Webster] to memory hath lent / A lasting fame, to raise his monument' (Commendatory Verses, 5–6, 7, 15–16, 37–8). From an early date, then, *The Duchess of Malfi* was regarded as Webster's greatest achievement; and even these early reactions display the correspondence between Webster and the grave which has remained such an influential view of the playwright.

Act One: Courtly Corruption and Commentary

The Duchess of Malfi, perhaps written with performance at the indoor Blackfriars theatre in mind, displays a much clearer use of the five-act structure than does *The White Devil* (which was perhaps composed for continuous performance – that is, with no intervals, in an outdoor theatre). Act One consists of a single, long scene set at the court of Malfi. As in *The White Devil*, Webster uses this scene to offer his audience a series of 'perspectives': the audience witnesses a variety of different interpretations of the courtly world, and also receives a series of different views of each of the main characters. Thus Webster's characteristic aesthetic relativism here becomes wedded to the content of his concerns.

Most of these views are initially provided by the commentary of Antonio and Delio, who are the first characters to appear on stage, and who initially appear to be peripheral to the action, observers of court life rather than full participants in it (it is only towards the end of the first act that the audience realises the central role Antonio will have in the action of the play). Antonio and Delio begin with a semi-abstract discussion of political philosophy: Antonio has just returned from the French court, and Delio is keen to hear what he has witnessed there. Antonio praises the behaviour of the prince, and this idealised (and absent) court is immediately established as the antithesis to the kind of courtly corruption which the audience will witness in Webster's Italy:

> . . . a prince's court
> Is like a common fountain, whence should flow
> Pure silver drops in general; but if't chance
> Some cursed example poison't near the head,
> *Death and diseases throughout the whole land spread.* (I, i, 11–15)

The play, it appears, will be interested in courtly politics; how a court should be managed, and whether or not the court of Malfi lives up to the example set by the court of France.

Antonio and Delio almost immediately turn from the mode of general discussion to observe specific individuals at this specific court (who are, nevertheless, frequently discussed in the terms of general 'types'). Bosola is 'the only court-gall' (I, i, 23, 'gall' meaning 'a satirical commentator') – yet:

> . . . he rails at those things he wants,
> Would be as lecherous, covetous, or proud,
> Bloody, or envious, as any man,
> If he had means to be so. (I, i, 25–8)

Immediately after this 'framing' introduction, the audience witnesses Bosola 'in action', involved in a dispute with the Cardinal over the former's lack of advancement in the court; 'Slighted thus? I will thrive some way', he vows (I, i, 57). When the Cardinal leaves the stage, Bosola joins Antonio and Delio to form a trio of commentators. His first target, predictably, is the Cardinal: 'Some fellows, they say, are possessed with the devil, but this great fellow were able to possess the greatest devil, and make him worse' (I, i, 44–6). Establishing the link between the church and the devil which will resound throughout the play, Bosola shifts his focus to the political power of Ferdinand, the Duke of Calabria and brother to the Cardinal (and, of course, to the Duchess of Malfi): the two brothers 'are like plum trees that grow crooked over standing pools; they are rich and o'erladen with fruit, but none but crows, pies, and caterpillars feed on them' (I, i, 48–51). Completing the move from the specific to the abstract – the reverse, of course, of the movement of Antonio and Delio's discussion – Bosola issues a warning about court life in general: 'places in the court are but like beds in the hospital, where this man's head lies at that man's foot, and so lower, and lower' (I, i, 65–8). On that comment, he exits the stage, whereupon he himself becomes the subject of comment by Antonio and Delio: emphasising the perspectival nature of Webster's dramatic construction, Delio 'knew this fellow seven years in the galleys / For a notorious murder' (I, i, 69–70), while Antonio has 'heard / He's very valiant' (I, i, 74–5).

In the opening lines, then, the audience has heard a variety of opinions on court life, from the positive report of the French court provided by Antonio, to the cynicism of Bosola. They have also witnessed some aspects of courtly life in action, with the relationships of power and authority on display in the relationship between Bosola and the Cardinal, and in the obsessive onlooking and commentary of Antonio, Delio and Bosola. They have also, through the conflicting comments on Bosola, become aware of the difficulty of making moral judgements in this courtly world. At this point, as Delio notes that 'the presence 'gins to fill' with courtiers (I, i, 82), a wider vision of the court of Malfi begins to come into view. The audience witnesses Ferdinand for the first time, engaged in a discussion about the roles and responsibilities of leadership; Castruchio, one of his advisors, suggests both that 'It is fitting a soldier arise to be a prince, but not necessary a prince descend to be a captain,' and that 'that realm is never long in quiet where the ruler is a soldier' (I, i, 95–6, 102–3). This voice, of apparent reason, is soon silenced by Ferdinand's claims of absolute authority in the court: 'Why do you laugh? Methinks you that are courtiers should be my touchwood, take fire when I give fire; that is, laugh when I laugh, were the subject never so witty' (I, i, 122–6). Given the discussion which opened the scene, the audience are invited to judge

Ferdinand against the models of courtly behaviour outlined by Antonio and Bosola; clearly, Ferdinand may appear to fall short of the ideal prince outlined by Antonio.

As the ongoing conversation is about horses, and as Antonio has a reputation for fine horsemanship, Ferdinand asks his opinion, another sign that the boundaries between observer and observed may on occasion be breached. After giving his answer, however, Antonio returns to his initial role as observer, responding to Delio's request for information about the Cardinal. Although the audience has already seen the Cardinal in conversation with Bosola, and has heard Bosola's negative characterisation of the churchman, Webster again provides conflicting views of one of his central characters through the commentary of Antonio and Delio. Delio, again, has heard much: 'They say he's a brave fellow, / Will play his five thousand crowns at tennis, dance, / Court ladies, and one that have fought single combat' (I, i, 153–5). While such characteristics may seem strange for a Cardinal, they certainly accord with the behaviour expected of a Courtier; Antonio, though, describing the Cardinal as a 'melancholy churchman' (I, i, 157–8), is concerned to stress his vulnerability to political and spiritual corruption:

> He should have been Pope, but instead of coming to it by the primitive decency of the church, he did bestow bribes so largely, and so impudently, as if he would have carried it away without heaven's knowledge. (I, i, 165–6)

Continuing in his role of commentator, Antonio provides a description of Ferdinand as possessing 'A most perverse and turbulent nature' (I, i, 169). In stark contrast, he then provides what is (it is worth remembering) the first extended description of the titular Duchess of Malfi. It bears quotation at some length, both for what it reveals to the audience about the Duchess, but also for what it might suggest about Antonio, the observer whom the audience has been encouraged to trust:

> But for their sister, the right noble Duchess:
> You never fixed your eye on three fair medals
> Cast in one figure, of so different temper.

For her discourse, it is so full of rapture
You only will begin then to be sorry
When she doth end her speech, and wish, in wonder,
She held it less vainglory to talk much
Than you penance to hear her. Whilst she speaks,
She throws upon a man so sweet a look
That it were able to raise one to a galliard
That lay in a dread palsy, and to dote
On that sweet countenance. But in that look
There speaketh so divine a continence
As cuts off all lascivious and vain hope.
Her days are practised in such noble virtue
That sure her nights – nay more, her very sleeps –
Are more in heaven than other ladies' shrifts. (I, i, 187–203)

There is much worth commenting upon in this passage, especially
given that the audience has seen the Duchess on stage, but has
not yet heard her speak. So, while Antonio begins by describing
the physical appearance of the Duchess (of 'one figure' with her
brothers), she is distinguished from them primarily by her powers
of speech. In contrast to the Renaissance ideal of the silent woman,
the Duchess's 'discourse' is 'full of rapture', so much so that an
audience will be sorry when she stops speaking. There is an erotic
element involved in Antonio's fixation on the Duchess's mouth,
emphasised for an early modern audience by the common cultural connection (misogynistically) assumed to exist between loose
female tongues, and loose female sexual organs. The power of her
speech and look to 'raise one [. . .] That lay in a dead palsy' then
becomes a power to 'raise' male sexual organs to a state of arousal.
Antonio seems to realise that he has unwillingly suggested this,
urging the 'continence' of the Duchess, and denying any 'lascivious' interpretation of his words. Nevertheless, his imagination then
shifts to the Duchess in bed at night, and although he is careful,
once again, to emphasise the virtue of the Duchess, nevertheless
there is a language of sin here: both 'shrift' and the earlier 'penance'
refer to the Roman Catholic practice of confession, suggesting that
Antonio may feel some – perhaps not fully realised – guilt about his
(voyeuristic) narration. So contradictory claims are made for both

the Duchess's sexual continence and her erotic powers of entice-
ment; at this point, having yet to hear the Duchess speak, the audience has no way of knowing if this is an 'accurate' representation
of the Duchess, or if it bespeaks something of Antonio's erotic fascination with this young widow. Certainly Delio's initial reaction
is that Antonio's keen powers of observation have abandoned him
at this point; the suggestion of disagreement between the two, of
course, may prompt the audience to reconsider the accuracy of the
information which these observers have previously related to them.

Having established in his audience's consciousness the suggestion of a significant relationship to unfold between Antonio and the
Duchess, Webster's focus returns to the figure of Bosola. Before
Bosola reappears, however, a conspiratorial moment between
Ferdinand and the Cardinal results in the latter recommending
Bosola's services as a spy to the former. Thus, when Ferdinand
offers gold to Bosola, the 'court-gall' is well aware that something
will be asked in return: 'What follows? [. . .] Whose throat must I
cut?' (I, i, 247–9). Ferdinand claims that he seeks Bosola's employment not as a murderer, but simply as a spy, his description of the
task at hand reinforcing the sense of the court as a system of closed
surveillance, already suggested by the obsessive observation and
comment of this first act:

> [. . .] I give you that
> To live i'th'court here, and observe the Duchess,
> To note all the particulars of her haviour,
> What suitors do solicit her for marriage
> And whom she best affects. (I, i, 251–5)

'Observe' and 'note': in many ways the key words of this first act,
Bosola would seem to need as little incentive to engage in these
acts as would Antonio, Delio or, for that matter, the audience, all
of whom have been involved in observing and noting from the
play's opening moments. Bosola, as he tends to do, complicates
matters further by linking the practice with the imagery of witchcraft and diabolism which has already begun to appear significant,
even at this early stage of the play: 'It seems you would create
me / One of your familiars [. . .] a very quaint invisible devil, in

flesh: / An intelligencer' (I, i, 257–61). Sensing that Bosola may be resisting his offer, Ferdinand falls back on the one strategy he knows he can rely on, the promise of social advancement: 'There is a place [that is, an office or role in the court] that I procured for you / This morning' (I, i, 268–9). Bosola accepts, while continuing to feel that such corruption is diabolical: 'Thus the devil / Candies all sins o'er' (I, i, 275–6). Ferdinand, cannily, suggests that all Bosola needs do is to continue as he has been behaving, thus implying that Bosola's cynicism and railing is in itself an affectation, a pose:

> Be yourself:
> Keep your old garb of melancholy; 'twill express
> You envy those that stand above your reach,
> Yet strive not to come near 'em. (I, i, 277–80)

'Be yourself': the injunction to maintain identity by the very act of pretending to be something one is not strikes at the core of the relationship between observer and observed so central to the dramaturgy of this act. If observation – intelligence, physiognomy – can provide all the answers, what room is there for an individual identity beyond external shows? Bosola's concluding line of this section – 'Sometimes the devil doth preach' (I, i, 291) – while recalling earlier descriptions of the Cardinal, also speaks an uncomfortable truth. It is not simply that the devil may seem to preach: that would rely on a contrast between a 'performed' exterior and an 'authentic' interior. Rather, by appearing to preach, the devil 'really' does.

There follows the Duchess's first extended action onstage and, significantly, she is physically and linguistically dominated by her brothers, both of whom attempt to persuade her against remarriage (even though neither suspects there is a specific suitor whom she is inclined to favour). Both draw on stereotypes of lustful and insatiate widows, and Ferdinand identifies the Duchess's social position as in itself hazardous to sexual morality: 'You live in a rank pasture here, i'th'court' (I, i, 306). Drawing on the play's already-introduced concern with reputation and legacy, Ferdinand argues for the importance of female chastity to both: 'There is a kind of honeydew that's deadly; / 'Twill poison your fame' (I, i, 307–8). 'Honeydew' (a sweet, sticky substance) may call to mind Bosola's earlier remarks about sins being 'candied' over, which then could link this moment to the earlier discourse – as enunciated by Antonio – of the sinfulness of sexuality; while Ferdinand's 'fame' here, and throughout the play, refers to both contemporary and posthumous reputation. Again, Ferdinand works here to achieve a culture of surveillance – and the fear associated with it – in the court: 'Your darkest actions – nay, your privat'st thoughts – / Will come to light' (I, i, 315–16). The Duchess's response, however, ironically echoes Ferdinand's earlier dismissal of Bosola's performance: 'I think this speech between you both was studied, / It comes so roundly off' (I, i, 329–30). Ferdinand, ever eager to have the last word, responds in kind, reminding the Duchess of her own performative tendencies, while also upping the ante, suggesting that performance itself may be inherently morally suspicious:

> I would have you to give o'er these chargeable revels;
> A visor and a mask are whispering-rooms
> That were ne'er built for goodness. (I, i, 333–5)

Briefly alone on stage after the exit of her two brothers, the Duchess tries to regain a voice of authentic individuality, in opposition to the pressures of family and society: 'If all my royal kindred / Lay in my way unto this marriage, / I'd make them my low footsteps' (I, i, 314–16). The image, while aiming to assert an individual will, also contains a note of arrogance, even self-importance. The imagined action recalls that of the central character in Christopher Marlowe's enormously successful play *Tamburlaine the Great*, who conquers kings in battle, and then uses them both as footstools, and as mock-horses to draw his chariot (one may recall here, of course, Webster's allusions in *The White Devil* to Shakespeare's *Hamlet*, another illustrious forebear; see p. 53). If the earlier play is indeed suggested by this image, then it is significant that the Duchess's attempts at establishing her individual will draw on exactly the kind of performative context which Ferdinand has just demonised. The Duchess, perhaps realising as much, metatheatrically imagines future generations recounting the narrative of her life: 'Let old wives report / I winked and chose a husband' (I, i, 348–9).

Such concerns – the inauthenticity of the self, the inescapability of performance and theatricality, the sinfully erotic nature of performance – have been skilfully set up by Webster to lead into the next 'micro-scene' of this extended scene: the wooing of Antonio by the Duchess. Ostensibly a scene of the exchange of the most private thoughts, the scene is configured as a performance from the very beginning, with the presence (known to the audience) of Cariola, the Duchess's waiting-woman, hidden behind an arras, listening and watching to all that unfolds. The levels of theatrical distancing effected by Webster, and the continuation from *The White Devil* of a perspectival approach to characterisation, mean that the audience is now close to being without a moral compass (aesthetic relativism in this case leading to moral relativism), and accordingly finds it difficult to know how the behaviour of Antonio and the Duchess in this scene should be judged. Is the Duchess, for example, inappropriately bawdy when she urges Antonio to 'use my ring' (I, i, 404; 'ring' being a common Renaissance euphemism for the female genitalia)? Is the act of the Duchess in placing the ring on Antonio's finger a profane symbol of the sexual encounter she is seeking, a spiritual symbol of what Antonio calls the 'first good deed began i'th'world / After man's creation, the sacrament of marriage' (I, i, 385–6), or both? What is clear is that the world of Malfi's court is a world in which meaning is always difficult to determine: when the Duchess describes herself as 'a wealthy mine' which she 'make[s] [Antonio] lord of' (I, i, 429–30), does the audience respond to the conventional gender hierarchy implied in the image, the challenge to conventional social hierarchies, or a complex mixture of both? The frustrating difficulty of determining meaning is outlined by the Duchess herself:

> [. . .] as a tyrant doubles with his words,
> And fearfully equivocates, so we
> Are forced to express our violent passions
> In riddles and in dreams. (I, i, 443–6)

Simultaneously acknowledging the deceptiveness and the necessity of performative representationalism, the Duchess rejects art and ceremony in favour of an emphasis on the bodily nature of identity:

> What is't distracts you? This is flesh and blood, sir;
> 'Tis not the figure cut in alabaster
> Kneels at my husband's tomb. Awake, awake, man!
> I do here put off all vain ceremony,
> And only do appear to you a young widow
> That claims you for her husband and, like a widow,
> I use but half a blush in't. (I, i, 453–9)

But, of course, these lines, spoken by a boy actor, raise as many problems related to the authenticity of identity as they can possibly hope to answer. Antonio's response – 'I will remain the constant sanctuary / of your good name' (I, i, 460–1) suggests an awareness that the actions of this scene may well have put that good name in question, as does the unconventional nature of the 'marriage' which follows. At this point, Cariola reveals herself, ceasing to be the audience of a scene from a romantic comedy, and becoming instead a witness of a quasi-legal ritual (despite, of course, the Duchess's claim to have 'put off all vain ceremony'). 'I have heard lawyers say,' claims the Duchess, 'a contract in a chamber / *Per verba de presenti* [that is, by speaking in one another's presence] is absolute marriage' (I, i, 478–9). This is, in fact, more or less how such clandestine marriages were broadly understood in early modern England: as legally binding. But the repeated protestations of the Duchess that this marriage is valid without a church ceremony – 'What can the church force more? [. . .] How can the church bind faster?' (I, i, 448–91) – certainly suggest an anxiety about the theological status of this marriage (an anxiety, of course, exacerbated by Antonio's earlier emphasis on the sinfulness of sexuality). The act ends with the Duchess asking Antonio to lead her 'by the hand, / Unto your marriage bed' (I, i, 495–6). The social and moral disorientation of the audience is encapsulated in the final words of the act, delivered by Cariola:

> Whether the spirit of greatness or of woman
> Reign most in her, I know not, but it shows
> A fearful madness. I owe her much of pity. (I, i, 504–6)

Act Two: 'Lice and Worms'

Webster uses the interval between acts in the indoor Blackfriars
theatre to allow for some fictional time to pass between the end
of Act One and the beginning of Act Two. Dramatically speaking, Act Two is structured very differently to Act One. Whereas
the first act imagined the Duchess's court as a semi-public space,
allowing characters to cross paths and meet in a single space across
the entirety of the act, by contrast Act Two stages a number of
short, intense scenes which generally take place in private rooms
or lodgings, under the cover of darkness, or in some other 'hidden'
manner. In this way, Webster both heightens the dramatic tension
of the piece, and begins the generic movement of the play from
a political tragedy of state (as it appears to be in Act One) to a
proto-gothic tragedy of supernatural horror.

Initially, the second act appears to begin where the first left
off, with Bosola, now apparently 'in character' as the malcontent
recommended by Ferdinand, discussing with Castruchio the qualities of 'an eminent courtier' (II, i, 1–2). The cynicism displayed
towards the courtly life here is soon extended to include a misogynistic outburst against female cosmetics – 'One would suspect it
[that is, a woman's closet] for a shop of witchcraft, to find in it
the fat of serpents, spawn of snakes, Jews' spittle, and their young
children's ordure – and all these for the face' (II, i, 38–40) – and
against women in general: 'I wonder you do not loathe yourselves'
(II, i, 46–7). Immediately, the misogyny extends itself to become a
far-reaching misanthropy:

> What thing is in this outward form of man
> To be beloved? [. . .]
> Though we are eaten up of lice and worms,
> And though continually we bear about us
> A rotten and dead body, we delight
> To hide it in rich tissue. All our fear –

Nay, all our horror – is lest our physician
Should put us in the ground, to be made sweet. (II, i, 48–63)

Such distaste for the body is in keeping with Bosola's garb of melancholy, and has the added effect of establishing him as an ideo-
logical antithesis to the Duchess, who had embraced her status as
'flesh and blood' at the end of the first act. When Bosola is left alone
on stage, and he steps back into the character of intelligencer, the
body becomes, not something that inspires a metaphysical disgust,
but rather, as in Act One, an object to be noted and observed:

[. . .] I observe our Duchess
Is sick o'days, she pukes, her stomach seethes,
The fins of her eyelids look most teeming blue,
She wanes i'th'cheek, and waxes fat i'th'flank,
And (contrary to our Italian fashion)
Wears a loose-bodied gown – there's somewhat in't! (II, i,
    66–71)

As has been noted, the character of the Duchess would have been
played by a boy actor; Webster's decision to place such emphasis
on the physiological changes in a woman's body occasioned by
pregnancy (this is the first of many references to the Duchess's
pregnant body) therefore highlights again the representational
limits of the early modern stage, and draws audience attention
again to the play's insistent questioning of both internal and
external definitions of human identity.

Antonio and Delio re-enter, and Bosola must once again assume
his role of malcontent. Webster's insistent questioning of the performative nature of identity again comes to the fore, however, in
Antonio's blunt declaration to Bosola, 'I do understand your inside'
(II, i, 86). Antonio's interpretation of Bosola's 'inside' continues:
'Because you would not seem to appear to the world puffed up with
your preferment, you continue this out-of-fashion melancholy' (II,
i, 88–90). Antonio is right, of course, that Bosola's 'out-of-fashion
melancholy' is an assumed role; but his interpretation of the reason
behind the performance is incorrect, and his supposition – that
there is a true 'inside' beneath the false 'melancholy' – has already

been demonstrated by the play to be naïve at best. Returning the insult, Bosola mocks Antonio's presumption to be 'chief man with the Duchess' (II, i, 100–1). Unknown to him, of course, the irony of Antonio's speech is also present in Bosola's.

There follows the entrance of the Duchess; as previously noted, Webster is at pains to draw attention to her pregnancy: she 'grow[s] fat', and is 'exceeding short-winded' (II, i, 112–13). Bosola continues with his quest to determine the pregnancy of the Duchess, noting that the carriage she requests is the same as the Duchess of Florence used 'when she was great with child' (II, i, 116), and offering her apricots, the desire for which was frequently interpreted as a sign of pregnancy. For Bosola, the Duchess's physiological appetites reveal her pregnancy, despite the fact that her clothing is explicitly designed to conceal her pregnant body (and, of course, to disguise the non-pregnant body of the boy actor):

A whirlwind strike off these bawd farthingales,
For, but for that and the loose-bodied gown,
I should have discovered apparently
The young springal cutting a caper in her belly. (II, i, 152–5)

'Apparently' here means visibly; the theatrical irony, of course, is that it is the 'farthingales' and 'loose-bodied gown' which create the femininity of the Duchess in the first place. Were they actually removed, Bosola (and the audience) would 'observe' a body physically incapable of sustaining the fiction of femininity. Webster, of course, is deliberately drawing the audience's attention to this tension, as the play's interrogation of identities continues. The scene ends with the Duchess being rushed off-stage, apparently entering into labour, and with some confusion among Antonio and Delio as to how to continue. Delio suggests that Antonio should 'Give out that Bosola hath poisoned her / With these apricocks' (II, i, 171–2), but Antonio displays an ominous lack of decisiveness: 'I am lost in amazement. I know not what to think on't' (II, i, 177).

Act Two, Scene Two stages the confused reaction of various characters onstage, while the Duchess gives birth offstage. The scene begins with Bosola in his role as intelligencer, considering his observations to himself: 'So, so: there's no question but her tetchiness and most vulturous eating of the apricocks are apparent signs of breeding' (II, ii, 1–3). Interrupted, he quickly shifts back to his role of misogynistic malcontent – 'the devil takes delight to hang at a woman's girdle, like a false, rusty watch, that she cannot discern how the time passes' (II, ii, 26–8). As the scene opens up to include more members of the court, the emphasis on gossip and observation again becomes clear: rumours are swirling about breaches of security, about the theft of valuables. Antonio, of course, along with the audience knows what is 'really' happening, and it is he who delivers the order which confines all the officers of the court to their chambers. But just as the previous scene ended with a hint of an unfavourable light being cast on Antonio, so too does this one. Delio, the voice of reason at this point, tries to calm Antonio's fears by urging him to reject superstitious interpretations of the natural world:

> How superstitiously we mind our evils!
> The throwing down salt, or crossing of a hare,
> Bleeding at nose, the stumbling of a horse,
> Or singing of a cricket, are of pow'r
> To daunt whole man in us. (II, ii, 77–81)

Delio's list of superstitious beliefs and behaviours is, clearly, an attempt to persuade Antonio of the foolishness and futility of such practices; yet no sooner has Antonio heard that the Duchess has given birth to a son, than he intends to cast a horoscope for the child: 'I'll presently / Go set a figure for's nativity' (II, ii, 87–8). Such a practice, though common in Renaissance England, was frequently criticised: the audience by this point may be wondering whether Antonio is still the knowledgeable observer he appeared to be in Act One.

Act Two, Scene Three continues the practice of the act by bringing Bosola on stage first. Building on the mention of superstition at the end of scene two, Webster begins here to create an atmosphere of menace and terror, thus encouraging the audience to *immediately* reconsider their negative attitude to Antonio's superstition: the audience disorientation so central to the dramatic

construction of *The White Devil* is beginning to make its presence
felt in this play as well:

> Sure I did hear a woman shriek. List, hah?
> [. . .] List again!
> It may be 'twas the melancholy bird,
> Best friend of silence and of solitariness,
> The owl, that screamed so. (II, iii, 1–9)

When Antonio enters, Bosola's reaction indicates that he seems
fearful and anxious: 'Put not your face and body / To such a
forced expression of fear [. . .] Methinks 'tis very cold, and yet
you sweat: you look wildly' (II, iii, 11–12, 19–20). As the tension
rises, the two men quickly fall to insults, Bosola calling Antonio 'a
false steward' and 'an impudent snake', and Antonio retorting with
'Saucy slave!' (II, iii, 35–8). Webster uses the rising tension here
to display Antonio's escalating susceptibility to superstition, and
his simultaneous (and largely unconvincing) desire to resist such
capitulation to unreason:

> [. . .] My nose bleeds.
> One that were superstitious would count
> This ominous, when it merely comes by chance.
> Two letters, that are wraught here for my name,
> Are drowned in blood!
> Mere accident! (II, iii, 41–6)

Because of his mental disintegration – one may be tempted to say
weakness – at this point, rather than because supernatural forces
really are conspiring against him, Antonio drops the 'nativity'
which he had cast for his son. If this lack of resolve – which contrasts with the steely determination of the Duchess – is Antonio's
flaw, then the flaw which makes the Duchess a tragic figure may
be the trust which she places in Antonio. In any case, the dropped
nativity allows Bosola to conclude that 'this precise fellow / Is the
Duchess bawd' (II, iii, 65–6), but does not allow him to identify
Antonio as the lover of the Duchess and father of her child. Having
found out at least some of the information he has been seeking – 'a

parcel of intelligency' – Bosola resolves to send letters to Rome, to inform Ferdinand and the Cardinal of his discovery.

At this point, the beginning of Act Two, Scene Four, the action switches to Rome; Webster immediately places the audience, however, not in the open spaces of Ferdinand's court, but in a private room belonging to the Cardinal. The play's emphasis on deception continues here, as Julia (a character who we meet for the first time at this point) has told her husband Castruchio that she has travelled to Rome 'to visit an old anchorite / Here, for devotion' (II, iv, 4–5); in reality, however, she has come because she has been seduced by the Cardinal, who delights in her deception – 'Thou art a witty false one' (II, iv, 5) – and then uses it as an example of the duplicity and changeability of all women: 'A man might strive to make glass malleable / Ere he should make them fixed' (II, iv, 14–15). Meanwhile, the audience hears that Bosola's letters have reached Ferdinand, who, according to one servant, has as a result gone 'out of his wits' (II, iv, 69). Delio, knowing of course something of the situation, voices a fear for Antonio – 'I do fear / Antonio is betrayed' (II, iv, 79–80) – which allows Webster to again clear the stage on an ominous note.

Act Two, Scene Five keeps the action in Rome; the location, now, though, is a private room of Ferdinand's, and the encounter is not the erotic one of the previous scene, but a council of power between Ferdinand and the Cardinal, each reacting to the news from Malfi. The Cardinal's is the more measured, politic response; Ferdinand's the more emotional and extreme: 'I am grown mad with't', he states (II, v, 2), confirming the servant's earlier description of him as 'out of his wits'. While certainly Ferdinand does seem fixated on his sister's sexuality – 'She's loose in the hilts, / Grown a notorious strumpet' (II, v, 85–6) – he is in this enacting in a different register the play's insistent (albeit ambivalent) emphasis on the body of the Duchess. And in his concern with rumour and reputation, he is again giving voice to a preoccupation with observation which the society represented in the play seems to share:

> Rogues do not whisper't now, but seek to publish't,
> As servants do the bounty of their lords,

> Aloud, and with a covetous, searching eye,
> To mark who note them. (II, v, 5–8)

Nevertheless, although he remains in tune with the dominant mood of the play, Ferdinand *does* threaten to take things too far; his images of violence display destructive tendencies:

> Would I could be one [that is, a tempest]
> That I might toss her palace 'bout her ears,
> Root up her goodly forests, blast her meads,
> And lay her general territory as waste
> As she hath done her honours. (II, v, 17–21)

This results in an urge to 'hew [. . .] her to pieces' (II, v, 31).

Yet there is, of course, another type of 'urge' present in Ferdinand in this scene; the insistent emphasis on the bodily sexuality of his sister has convinced many critics that Ferdinand harbours incestuous desires for his sister, which he may or (more likely) may not have admitted to himself. (Incest was not an uncommon theme in Jacobean drama, and some plays portray an incestuous brother-sister relationship in much more detail than *The Duchess of Malfi*: John Ford's *'Tis Pity She's a Whore* is an excellent example.) This would begin to explain why Ferdinand's reaction is more extreme than that of the Cardinal, and why he seems compelled to visualise his sister's sexual encounters:

> [. . .] Talk to me somewhat, quickly,
> Or my imagination will carry me
> To see her in the shameful act of sin.
> [. . .] Happily with some strong-thighed bargeman,
> Or one o'th'woodyard, that can quoit the sledge
> Or toss the bar, or else some lovely squire
> That carries coals up to her privy lodgings. (II, v, 39–45)

The Cardinal, shocked by Ferdinand's lack of self-restraint, urges him to compose himself: 'There is not in nature / A thing that makes man so deformed, so beastly, / As doth intemperate anger [. . .] Come, put yourself / In tune' (II, v, 56–62). Ferdinand's reply, again in keeping with the play's emphasis on the performed nature of identity, is suitably ambiguous: 'I will only study to seem / The thing that I am not' (II, v, 62–3). It is only the length of a couple of lines, however, until he returns to forming ingenious plans for the violent torture of the Duchess and her lover (the identity of whom, of course, is still unknown to Ferdinand):

> [. . .] I would have their bodies
> Burnt in a coal-pit, with the ventage stopped,
> That their cursed smoke might not ascend to heaven;
> Or dip the sheets they lie in in pitch and sulphur,
> Wrap them in't, and then light them like a match;
> Or else to boil their bastard to a cullis,
> And give't his lecherous father, to renew
> The sin of his back. (II, v, 66–73)

The progressive darkening of the atmosphere of the play which has been one of the main dramatic functions of Act Two is now almost complete: the act ends with Ferdinand vowing to 'fix' the Duchess 'in a general [that is, total] eclipse' (II, v, 79).

Act Three: From Comedy to Tragedy

Act Three, Scene One recalls the opening of the first act by commencing with the on-stage meeting of Antonio and Delio, although this time it is Delio, rather than Antonio, who has been absent from the court. It also recalls the opening of the second act by drawing attention to the time that has passed in the act interval; since the end of Act Two, the Duchess 'hath had two children more, a son and a daughter' (III, i, 7). Delio's response, 'I should dream / It were within this half-hour' (III, i, 11), maintains the metatheatrical joke. But if the scene opens on a lighthearted note, the tone soon darkens considerably, as Antonio outlines the spread of rumour and public censure regarding the Duchess: 'The common people do directly say / She is a strumpet' (III, i, 26). Ferdinand and the Duchess come on stage, and Ferdinand tests the veracity of the rumours by informing the Duchess that he has identified a suitable husband for her; the Duchess's response

'Fie upon him' (III, i, 41), convinces Ferdinand that 'Her guilt treads on / Hot-burning coulters' (III, i, 56–7). Left on stage with just Bosola, the scene changes tone again to stage a conspiratorial moment; Bosola, at the instigation of Ferdinand, has got hold of 'a false key / Into her bedchamber' (III, i, 80–1). Ferdinand's plan to use the 'key' highlights both the potentially incestuous nature of his fixation on his sister, and the violation of 'private' space which the play stages so forcefully.

The second scene of the act, one of the most celebrated in Webster's oeuvre, stages the very violation of the privacy of the bedchamber foretold at the end of Act Three, Scene One. Like its predecessor, however, the scene opens with a jocular tone, the light-hearted jests between Antonio, Cariola, and the Duchess provoking the last to proclaim 'I prithee, / When were we so merry?' (III, ii, 52–3). When Antonio and Cariola leave the stage, intending a kind of practical joke on the Duchess, Webster again enacts a violent change of atmosphere, typical of the aesthetic relativism informing both this play and *The White Devil*. Ferdinand's entrance to the chamber is at first not noticed by the Duchess, who continues to speak to Antonio and Cariola, unaware of their absence (thus, of course, revealing that she has been sharing her bed). Her only form of defence against the accusatory stares of Ferdinand is to claim 'I am married' (III, ii, 82). This, of course, has no effect on the Duke, who hands her a dagger (its phallic shape recalling the 'false key' of the previous scene), and instigates the imagery of imprisonment ('I would have thee build / Such a room [. . .] as our anchorites / To holier use inhabit' (III, ii, 101–3)) which will build throughout the remainder of the play. Soon after Ferdinand's furious exit, Bosola enters; to him, the Duchess, hoping to save Antonio, concocts a story about Antonio's fraudulent managing of the court finances. Arranging a safe haven for Antonio in Ancona, she publicly accuses him of financial mismanagement, expels him from her service, and thus gives him an opportunity to flee. This leaves Bosola and the Duchess on stage together. The former, suspecting 'cunning' (III, ii, 172), praises Antonio's virtues to the Duchess; as a result, she confides the fact of their clandestine marriage, and the scene ends with Bosola convincing the Duchess to make a false pilgrimage to the Marian shrine at Loreto (with the true purpose of visiting

Antonio) and then informing the audience of his plan to 'reveal /
All to my lord' (III, ii, 328–9). Thus the swift generic turn from
comedy to tragedy in Act Three, Scene One is repeated in an even
more dizzying manner in Act Three, Scene Two.

After the relative length of Act Three, Scene Two, the following scene begins by outlining the Cardinal's plan to return to his
role as a soldier, and proceeds with the familiar courtly commentary of Delio and other onlookers. A short scene, the atmosphere
nevertheless changes halfway through with the entrance of Bosola,
informing both the Cardinal and Ferdinand of all that he knows.
Thus the turning point of the play is reached, as the clandestine
nature of the Duchess's marriage is revealed, and the characters
onstage become aware of what the audience has known all along.

Act Three, Scene Four momentarily shifts the mode of the play
from conspiratorial intrigue to dramatic spectacle. Set at the shrine
to the Virgin Mary in Loreto, the scene reveals both Webster's
dramatic interest in the ritual and ceremony of Catholicism, and
simultaneously suggests the Virgin as possible dramatic type
standing behind, and therefore commenting on, the figure of the
Duchess in the play. The scene is framed by the commentary of
two unnamed pilgrims, who prepare the audience for the change
in dramaturgy with the phrase 'I expect / A noble ceremony' (III,
iv, 6–7). The ceremony in question is the Cardinal's replacement
of an ecclesiastical identity with a military one; this ceremony
is performed in a spectacular fashion, with music and elaborate
ritual presented on stage, recalling the installation of the Pope in
Webster's earlier *The White Devil*. Immediately, Webster employs
another dramatic technique which he had used to great effect in the
earlier play, that of the dumb show. Here, the dumbshow is used to
reveal to the audience the banishment of Antonio, the Duchess, and
their children from the state of Ancona. The unnamed pilgrims,
continuing to observe the scene, suggest possible interpretations
to the audience, some supporting the Duchess – 'the Cardinal /
Bears himself much too cruel' (III, iv, 26–70) – others appearing to
blame her for poor judgment: 'who would have thought / So great
a lady would have matched herself / Unto so mean a person?' (III,
iv, 24–6). Their final words, moreover, encourage the audience to
believe that the generic turn to tragedy, hinted at throughout this

act, is now complete: 'Fortune makes this conclusion general: / All things do help th'unhappy man to fall' (III, iv, 43–4).

This impression is confirmed by the next scene, Act Three, Scene Five. While the general dramatic construction of the act has been to enact and re-enact the move from comedy to tragedy in each scene, this scene – sombre throughout – marks the irrevocable move of the act to a tragic structure. Whereas the act began with Antonio commenting on the expanding family possessed by he and the Duchess, it ends with the division of that family, Antonio and their eldest son flying to Milan (repeating, of course, the unhappy flight to Ancona of the previous scene), and the Duchess and their remaining two children imprisoned by Bosola under orders from Ferdinand. The looming presence of the grave begins to be clearly felt in the parting of Antonio and the Duchess, as the latter proclaims:

> Let me look upon you once more, for that speech
> Came from a dying father. Your kiss is colder
> Than that I have seen an holy anchorite
> Give to a dead man's skull. (III, v, 87–90)

The imagery employed by the Duchess suggests her awareness that she is now playing a tragic part; this is emphasised again just a few lines later:

> When Fortune's wheel is overcharged with princes,
> The weight makes it move swift. I would have my ruin
> Be sudden (III, v, 96–8)

The one exception to this move to a tragic mode comes in the Duchess's final speech, with the line 'There's no deep valley, but near some great hill' (III, v, 144); but even this seems to be less an envisioning of a tragicomic reversal of fortune, than a stoic acceptance of death, and a hope for posthumous renown.

Act Four: The 'Gothic'

If Act Three represents a generic movement of the play from tragedy to comedy, the beginning of Act Four reveals that it is a very specific type of tragedy which Webster has in mind. Although the term would not come into use until much later, Webster here presents his audience with a prototype of the 'Gothic' scenario popular in later centuries. The Duchess is, of course, suffering 'imprisonment', as Ferdinand himself reminds us (IV, i, 2); and Ferdinand's visit to the Duchess takes place 'i'th'night,' when 'neither torch nor taper / Shine[s]' (IV, i, 24–6). For Ferdinand, the darkness is symbolic of what he perceives as the Duchess's sinfulness – 'This darkness suits you well' (IV, i, 30) – although an audience may well view the darkness as equally revealing of Ferdinand's own psychological state. The darkness is also instrumental in Ferdinand's plan to induce despair in the Duchess, first by presenting her with a dead man's hand, and then arranging the revelation of what Webster's stage directions call '*the figures of Antonio and his children, appearing as if they were dead*' (IV, i, 55SD). Both properties make the Duchess think, not just of the death of her family, but of the supernatural, setting the tone for much of what follows: the severed hand makes her exclaim against Ferdinand's 'witchcraft' (IV, i, 54), while the wax figures (which, of course, she believes to be the real corpses of Antonio and the children), call to mind the wax figures reportedly used by witches:

> It wastes me more
> Than were't my picture, fashioned out of wax,
> Stuck with a magical needle, and then buried
> In some foul dunghill; (IV, i, 62–5)

The spectacles have the desired effect of making the Duchess wish for death, as she again draws attention to her complicated status as the female hero of a dramatic tragedy: 'I account this world a tedious theatre, / For I do play a part in't 'gainst my will' (IV, i, 84–5); 'say I long to bleed: It is some mercy, when men kill with speed' (IV, i, 109–10). In part, Webster is here perhaps preparing the audience for the unconventionally early death of his tragedy's title-character. The scene ends with Ferdinand planning more torments for his captive sister – 'I will send her masques of common courtesans / Have her meat served up by bawds and ruffians' (IV, i, 124–5) – and Bosola repenting his role in the torment (suggesting, clearly, to the audience that their sympathy at this point should lie with the plight of the Duchess).

Act Four, Scene Two operates in similar dramatic terms to Act Four, Scene One, with the Duchess still imprisoned, and facing a range of torments devised by Ferdinand. The proto-Gothic tone and atmosphere of this scene are clear from the Duchess's opening line: 'What hideous noise was that?' (IV, ii, 1). Cariola suspects that it is the 'consort / Of madmen' which Ferdinand has arranged to visit the Duchess, and the progression of the scene proves her correct (IV, ii, 2–3). But before the madmen make their appearance, Webster takes pains to once again empha- sise the Duchess's awareness of the fate which generic necessity has determined for her: 'Discourse to me some dismal tragedy' (IV, ii, 8); 'Fortune seems only to have her eyesight / To behold my tragedy' (IV, ii, 35–6). The entrance of the madmen, when it comes, is accompanied by a musical spectacle markedly differ- ent to that of the Cardinal's installation as a soldier at Loreto, to which it serves as a kind of counterpoint. Whereas 'churchmen' sang the earlier song, here a 'madman' sings '*to a dismal kind of music*' (IV, ii, 60SD). There follows a dance of the madmen, with more music.

If the Duchess is constantly aware, in this act, of the tragic nature of the role she is playing, nevertheless the dramaturgy of the play seems determined to also fix her in the place of an audi- ence, witnessing a series of dramatic spectacles. After the figures of Antonio and the children, and the masque of the madmen, Bosola (the consummate actor) enters in disguise as an old man, claiming to be a 'tomb-maker', and thus keeping the death of the Duchess at the forefront of the audience's attention (IV, ii, 140). The Duchess's response to Bosola – 'I am Duchess of Malfi still' (IV, ii, 134) has occasioned much critical debate regarding the tone in which it should be delivered; what should not be overlooked is that it is Bosola's ruminations on death and decay which comprise the majority of lines spoken in this part of the scene.

The next 'entertainment' to be sent on stage to the Duchess is a team of executioners, carrying their stage properties of '*a coffin, cords and a bell*' (IV, ii, 156SD). Bosola, still on stage, nevertheless changes his role in the dramatic torment unfolding in front of the Duchess: 'I am the common bellman / That usually is sent to condemned persons / The night before they suffer' (IV, ii, 164–6). But of course, the dramatic scene enacted in front of the Duchess is no longer fictional: the wax figures may not have been real, but the madmen were madmen, and the executioners are really executioners. Thus the Duchess's sense that she is a figure in a tragic play comes true: she is strangled on stage, while orders are given to kill the children off-stage.

After the execution of the Duchess, the children, and Cariola, Ferdinand enters and, on seeing the Duchess's dead body, almost immediately begins to feel remorse, blaming Bosola, and refusing him the reward which had been previously promised for the deed. Seeming distracted – 'I'll go hunt the badger by owl-light' (IV, ii, 326) – Ferdinand exits, leaving Bosola on stage with the body of the Duchess. Unexpectedly, the Duchess recovers just long enough for Bosola to inform her that Antonio and the children are still alive. Weeping after her death, Bosola undertakes to fulfil the Duchess' last request, to deliver her lifeless body 'to the reverent dispose / Of some good women' (IV, ii, 363–4). Thus the fourth act ends with the Duchess dead, leaving the final act to be an almost entirely masculine affair.

Act Five: A Just Revenge?

Act Five, like acts one and three, begins with a conversation between Antonio and Delio; thus Webster counters the traumatic event at the end of Act Four with a familiar stage image, even as that image recalls the descent into tragedy at the end of Act Three, the last act to open in this fashion. The scene, though short, has a number of important dramatic functions: it establishes that Antonio does not yet know of the Duchess's death; it serves to reinforce, through the comments of Delio, how little chance there is of Ferdinand and the Cardinal forgiving Antonio; and it establishes that Antonio is now penniless, his lands having been seized by order of the Cardinal. Perhaps most importantly, the scene develops the distraction suggested by the strangeness of Ferdinand's exit at the end of Act Four. Through the figure of Pescara (briefly sketched as a noble and honourable aristocrat, in marked contrast to Ferdinand and the Cardinal), Webster can inform his audience that 'Prince Ferdinand's come to Milan / Sick, as they give out, of an apoplexy; / But some say 'tis a frenzy' (V, i, 59). Thus the scene is set for Ferdinand's madness, mirroring that of the madmen in Act Four; and one repetition is followed by another, as Antonio outlines his plan to 'visit [the Cardinal], about the mid of night, / As once his brother did our noble Duchess' (V, i, 66–7). Thus one of the central dramatic techniques of Act Five – repetition, mirroring, *echoing* – is set in place immediately.

Act Five, Scene Two opens with the first onstage vision of the madness of Ferdinand, described by a doctor as lycanthropia, understood – characteristically for the sceptical Webster – as a psychological, rather than a supernatural, disease: 'In those that are possessed with't, there o'erflows / Such melancholy humour, they imagine / Themselves to be transformèd into wolves' (V, ii, 8–10). The wolf, of course, has been a constant verbal figure in the play, particularly in the torture scenes of Act Four, so it is dramatically fitting that this is the form Ferdinand's mental torture takes. Ferdinand himself does not display his lycanthropia, but does display an extreme emotionalism and impatience, which the other characters take as evidence of his madness. As the stage empties following the exit of Ferdinand, the Cardinal and Bosola are the only characters left. The Cardinal feigns ignorance of the Duchess's death, urging Bosola to kill Antonio, apparently so that the Duchess will be free to marry again. Rapidly following this action, Julia, as part of a plan to seduce Bosola, convinces the Cardinal to admit his role in the murder of the Duchess; Julia is poisoned by the Cardinal, but not before Bosola has become privy to the confession. Both in a difficult position, Bosola and the Cardinal form a league of sorts; when the Cardinal leaves the stage, however, Bosola makes it clear to the audience that his true sympathies lie with Antonio, and suggests that this play may lurch towards the conventions of revenge tragedy at the finale, as did *The White Devil*: 'It may be / I'll join with thee in a most just revenge' (V, ii, 337–8).

Act Five, Scene Three is, of course, the 'echo scene', one of the most evocative scenes in the Webster canon, and one which presents some serious difficulties in determining the original staging techniques used. The opening stage direction indicates that '*there is an echo from the Duchess's grave*' (V, iii, 0SD), which may indicate that the voice of the echo was supplied by the boy actor who had played the part of the Duchess. The ostensible setting, however, is near 'the Cardinal's window' (V, iii, 1), built on 'the ruins of an ancient abbey' (V, iii, 2). The play, of course, is set in Italy, and the ruins may well be 'ancient'; but to an English audience the 'abbey' and the 'cloister' may well suggest the long-disused monasteries of Catholic England, in which case Antonio's nostalgic reverie for the ruins troubles any sense of Webster as an anti-Catholic writer. In any case, the function of the scene is clear: to suggest a supernatural presence, warning Antonio about the dangers of his plan. It is very easy to overlook the rarity of genuinely 'supernatural' moments in Webster's drama; almost always, supernatural apparitions can be explained either as malicious tricks or as psychological disturbances. Even the echo scene can be read 'straight' – as simply an echo of Antonio's voice. But the tone and effect of this scene in performance is often markedly different to the nativity scene, for example; and it seems that Webster – following his creed of aesthetic relativism – is here licensing himself to use the suggestion of a ghostly visitation to achieve the desired emotional effect on the audience.

Act Five, Scene Four, set in the Cardinal's lodging, is a scene of darkness, recalling both the visit of Ferdinand to the Duchess's chamber in Act Three, and the scene in Act Four of the Duchess's murder. Where darkness in those scenes represented horror, here it also represents confusion: both the distracted mind of Ferdinand, who enters briefly, displaying signs of his madness, and the confusion of Bosola who, attempting to kill the Cardinal, instead stabs Antonio in the dark. The repetition of the earlier scenes means that Antonio's death demands to be seen as a parodic version of the death of the Duchess; instead of facing his death in a stoic fashion, Antonio is unexpectedly stabbed in the dark. And whereas the Duchess ends life by embracing her aristocratic identity – 'I am Duchess of Malfi still' – Antonio ends his life by rejecting it: 'let my son fly the courts of princes' (V, iii, 71). Thus the projected revenge of Antonio and Bosola ends unexpectedly with the death of Antonio at the hands of the very man who had vowed to help him.

Act Five, Scene Five nevertheless sees Bosola carry out his threat to become the play's avenger, stabbing and wounding both the Cardinal and Ferdinand, but not escaping his own death at the hands of Ferdinand. Bosola, then, carries responsibility for the deaths of all the main characters in the play, yet still ends the play a figure of considerable complexity, much more than a stock villain. And it is in many ways Bosola who, at the play's end, recalls most clearly the figure of the Duchess; his sense that Antonio died by 'Such a mistake as I have often seen / In a play' (V, v, 94–5) recalls the Duchess's frequent comparison of herself to a tragic figure, while his claim that 'We are only like dead walls, or vaulted graves, / That, ruined, yields no echo' (V, v, 96–7), clearly recalls, even as it serves as a counterpoint to, the echo from the Duchess's grave in Act Five, Scene Three. The play ends with the establishment of a new generation in power, as Delio enters with the son of Antonio and the Duchess, the consensus being that this son will take over the rule of the court. But this, of course, clearly goes against Antonio's dying wish, while Delio's rumination on the fate of 'great men' does not appear to bode well for the new Duke of Malfi:

> These wretched eminent things
> Leave no more fame behind 'em than should one
> Fall in a frost, and leave his print in snow;
> As soon as the sun shines, it ever melts,
> Both form and matter. (V, v, 112–16)

CRITICAL HISTORY

Monumentalisation

As noted in the previous section, the earliest surviving comments on *The Duchess of Malfi* are to be found in the earliest printed edition of the play, the quarto of 1623. Middleton's poem is the first reference to the play as a 'masterpiece of tragedy'; and

Middleton's tribute to the play takes the form of a conscious re-enactment of what must already have seemed clearly Websterian concerns:

> Thy monument is raised in thy life-time;
> And 'tis most just; for every worthy man
> Is his own marble. (Hunter and Hunter 1969: 33)

It is worth noting that the language of the grave here is not perceived as forbiddingly morbid, in the way that it would be by critics of later centuries; rather, Middleton applauds Webster's interest in posthumous glory and renown, going so far to suggest that the *Duchess* itself is Webster's lasting monument. William Rowley's poetic response to the play, on the other hand, though enthusiastic, is a much less accomplished piece of poetry: 'I never saw thy duchess till the day / That she was lively body'd in thy play' (Hunter and Hunter 1969: 34). Although this is not a great poem in itself, it does remind us that the Jacobeans responded enthusiastically to *The Duchess* as a performance first and foremost, rather than as a literary text (the text was not published until nine years after the initial staging); this is significant for analysing the responses of later critics, who often tried to make a distinction between Webster the successful poet, and Webster the failed playwright. The final poem in the volume, that of John Ford, follows the Middletonian example by praising Webster in the very terms which he himself would have found most appealing: 'Crown him a poet, whom nor Rome, nor Greece, / Transcend in all theirs, for a masterpiece' (Hunter and Hunter 1969: 34). In this Renaissance culture, of course, comparison to the ancient Greeks and Romans is the greatest praise possible, even though Webster's classicism was much less overt than some of his contemporaries. Again, though, the term 'masterpiece' makes an appearance here, both Middleton and Ford recognising, as many subsequent generations of critics were to do, the claim of *The Duchess* to be Webster's most successful piece of work; and the later use of the words 'memory', 'fame', and 'monument' all suggest that Ford was as sympathetic to Webster's dramatic exploration of these concerns as was Middleton, his fellow playwright.

'Against the Laws of the Scene': Negative Views

Unfortunately, apart from these three poems, there is relatively little comment on *The Duchess of Malfi* which has survived from the seventeenth century. We do have the hand-written comments of a man called Abraham Wright, writing in his commonplace book around the year 1650. As the theatres were closed between 1642 (the outbreak of the Civil War) and 1660 (the Restoration of the monarchy), Wright must almost certainly have encountered the play as a primarily literary, rather than dramatic, artefact. His comments, interestingly, are much less enthusiastic than those of Middleton and Ford: 'A good play, especially for the plot at the latter end, otherwise plain [. . .] And which is against the laws of the scene, the business was two years a-doing' (Hunter and Hunter 1969: 35). Of interest here is the castigation of Webster for violating the neo-classical unities, something which would make his plays unpopular among eighteenth-century readers and audiences; it is notable, however, that this castigation first becomes apparent when the play is removed from its original performance conditions. Not only is there nothing unusual or remarkable in English Renaissance plays dramatising action which takes place over a period of some years, Webster structures his play according to the conditions of performance in the Blackfriars playhouse, so that these long spaces of time always occur when the stage is cleared, and music played between the acts.

The last significant reference to the play in the seventeenth century comes in the diary of Samuel Pepys, who both read the play and saw it performed, and seems to have had different experiences with each form of media. Over this period of six years (1662–68), Pepys seems to have had mixed reactions to the play as performed, describing it as 'well performed' in 1662 (admittedly without any real enthusiasm) but as a 'sorry play' in 1668 (though he seems more concerned about his company at the playhouse on this occasion) (Hunter and Hunter 1969: 37–8). Yet clearly the play was being performed relatively frequently in Restoration London, and was finding a popular audience in its textual form as well.

Given the nature of his work, it is unsurprising that the

neoclassical literary milieu of eighteenth-century London had little time for Webster; indeed, references to the playwright seem to have been scant at this time. One exception is in the work of the playwright Lewis Theobald who, in a manner reminiscent of Abraham Wright in the mid-seventeenth century, castigates Webster for his apparently cavalier disregard for aesthetic and dramatic decorum: 'As for rules, he either knew them not or thought them too servile a restraint' (Hunter and Hunter 1969: 41). Theobald, at least, acknowledges that the dramatic Unities were not as important to Renaissance playwrights as they were to those of the eighteenth century; but even this is not enough to spare Webster, who is taken, as he would often be in the nineteenth century as well, as the extreme example of everything that was wrong with the Jacobean playwrights.

Gothic Horror

As this book has argued in the chapter on *The White Devil*, it is in the nineteenth century – and particularly in the midst of a Romantic fascination with the Gothic – that critics really begin to make Webster a focus of serious critical discussion (and, often, of controversy). This is as true of *The Duchess of Malfi* as it is of the earlier play. Charles Lamb is the first writer to really take Webster seriously as a writer of horror and terror:

> To move a horror skilfully, to touch a soul to the quick, to lay upon fear as much as it can bear, to wean and weary a life till it is ready to drop, and then step in with mortal instruments to take its last forfeit – this only a Webster can do. (Hunter and Hunter 1969: 37)

Lamb's enthusiasm for Webster's art is apparent here, and it may be no surprise that in an age when Gothic fiction was immensely popular, the proto-Gothic stylings of Webster would find some significant champions. It is also significant, in this age of literary Romanticism, that Lamb outlines the individuality of Webster ('this only a Webster can do'): one of the most common claims for Webster's importance among critics writing in the nineteenth and twentieth centuries is just this sense that his is a unique voice, one that can not be replicated or imitated by other writers.

This sense of Webster as the poet of terror also found favour with R. H. Horne, who resuscitated the play for performance in the 1850s: 'if the two chief elements of tragic power be terror and pity, assuredly both of these are carried to the highest degree in *The Duchess of Malfi*' (Hunter and Hunter 1969: 58). Yet Horne's Lamb-like appreciation of the play's powers of terror is nevertheless matched by a Theobaldian sense of the dramatic and structural limitations of the play as a work for the stage. It is worth quoting at length from Horne, to illustrate both what the nineteenth century thought were the necessary qualities for a play to possess (and what, correspondingly, it felt the *Duchess* was lacking), and to analyse the particular imagery which Horne employs to describe the play:

> It hence became apparent that if this great tragedy was to be exhumed from its comparative obscurity, by representation on the stage, all the characters must be made consistent with themselves, and all the events proper to them – all the parts must be made coherent – and all this be built with direct relationship to the whole, and direct tendency to the final results. Yet, amidst all this the great scenes must be religiously preserved, or I should do worse than nothing, and produce a weak and sacrilegious deformity. What I have, therefore, sought to do, is as though a grand old abbey – haunted, and falling into decay – stood before me, and I had undertaken to reconstruct it anew with as much of its own materials as I could use – asking pardon for the rest – but preserving almost entire its majestic halls and archways, its loftiest turrets, its most secret and solemn chambers, where the soul, in its hours of agony, uplifted its voice to God. (Hunter and Hunter 1969: 59)

Although a remarkable passage, this is nevertheless in many ways consistent with a certain type of nineteenth-century thinking about Webster. The first thing to notice, of course, is how Webster's dramaturgy does not accord with Horne's view of what a successful play should be like: Horne stresses the importance of consistency and coherence, both of which he finds notably lacking in Webster's (aesthetically relativist) approach to stagecraft. But the second half of the passage is even more interesting for what it tells us about this view of the play. *The Duchess of Malfi* is likened to 'a grand old abbey': it is itself a Gothic relic, similar to the ruined abbey in the echo scene of the play. This is no longer, it seems, a living theatrical text, but rather a romanticised relic from a bygone age, which must be brought back to life (in the manner, perhaps, of Frankenstein's creature). Thus critics like Horne and Lamb display a clear interest in the proto-Gothic qualities of the play's final two acts, but much less interest in the dramatic and generic experimentation which Webster undertakes in Acts One, Two, and Three.

If Lamb and Horne were impressed by *The Duchess of Malfi*, the same cannot be said for Charles Kingsley who, writing in 1856, accused Webster of 'thinking and writing of [. . .] not truth, but effect' (Hunter and Hunter 1969: 62–3). The Gothic terrors of Act Four have little impact on this writer, other than, it seems, to leave a feeling of distaste:

> The prison-scenes between the Duchess and her tormentors are painful enough, if to give pain be a dramatic virtue; and she appears in them really noble; and might have appeared far more so, had Webster taken half as much pains with her as he has with the madmen, ruffians, ghosts, and screech-owls in which his heart really delights. (Hunter and Hunter 1969: 63–4)

Thus Kingsley represents the obverse of the enthusiasm of Lamb and Horne; where the latter pair see a skilful manipulation of the audience's emotions to achieve the desired effects of terror and pity (presumably, although this is never explicitly spelled out, to achieve a kind of Aristotelian carthasis), Kingsley sees only a shameful purveyor of cheap tricks, a kind of fairground horror-show (to use an anachronistic metaphor). Implicit here is a sche-matisation of aesthetic experience into discrete categories, some of which are intrinsically more valuable than others: Aristotelian catharsis is more acceptable – is *better for you* – than the voyeuristic thrills of carnival. But Webster, as I have argued, does not share this conceptual codification – different types of dramatic spectacle produce different types of aesthetic experience, but the privileging of any one of these experiences is inappropriate. Websterian drama is disorientating in its effect on a spectator: it utilises terror in a variety of ways, not just in an Aristotelian fashion. So the battle-lines over the value of *The Duchess of Malfi* were clearly drawn by the middle years of the nineteenth century; and they were prima-rily over the interpretation of the horrors of the fourth and fifth acts.

Stagecraft and Morality

Although the twentieth century inherited many of its values and concerns from the nineteenth century, the rapidity with which these values changed can be traced in literary criticism as in other forms of cultural production. This book's chapter on *The White Devil* has already discussed the significance of T. S. Eliot's appro-priation of the figure of Webster in 'Whispers of Immortality'; and much of what has been said about the influence of this poem on views of *The White Devil* can also be said about *The Duchess of Malfi*. So, writing in 1947, M. C. Bradbrook was still focusing on the prison scenes of the play, and still concerned with Webster's techniques of horror. However, the need to justify such an interest, so pronounced in the nineteenth-century critics, no longer seems to be as important:

> The horror of Webster's play depends upon a powerful sense of the supernatural combined with a scepticism far deeper than that of professed rebels like Marlowe. An intense capac-ity for feeling and suffering, within a clueless intellectual maze, springs from the deepened insight into character which was Webster's greatest strength as a dramatist. (Hunter and Hunter 1969: 133)

This is a markedly different response to Webster even from the enthusiasm of Charles Lamb; the emphasis on Webster's powers of characterisation is distinct from the critical discussion of the nineteenth century; and the cathartic effect of the suffering on the audience, so significant to Lamb and Horne, is much less pronounced in Bradbrook, albeit still implicit.

This view – that Webster was not just a great poet or a master of horror, but also an innovative and original dramatist – becomes increasingly popular in critical discussion not just of *The White Devil*, as has already been argued, but also of *The Duchess of Malfi*. In an influential article on *The Duchess* published in 1958, for example, Inga-Stina Ekeblad argued that 'Webster – though he often leaves us in confusion – does at his most intense achieve such a fusion, creating something structurally new and vital' (Hunter and Hunter 1969: 204). The twentieth century was, of course, an age of intense theatrical experiment, just as the early modern period had been; and it may be that this contributed to the increased willingness to view Webster's dramatic experimentation in a more positive light, to view his dramatic techniques – his aesthetic relativism, even if not always formally acknowledged as such – as innovative and significant, rather than as failures. Certainly the 'blurring' of forms and genres, and disregard for conventional structures and characterisations, speaks more clearly to the theatrical conventions of the twentieth century than to those of the eighteenth and nineteenth.

Similarly, James L. Calderwood, writing in 1962, argued that an attention to the dramatic techniques of *The Duchess of Malfi* could help critics make more sense of some of the old arguments surrounding Webster's skill as a dramatist, and the nature of his moral schema: 'Webster, far from failing to present an "internal scale to measure depravity," is entirely willing to test evil against good [. . .] Webster's use of ceremony helps to clarify some of the rather vexing problems of action, motivation, and character' (Hunter and Hunter 1969: 268). According to this view, Webster is a moralist, interested in questions of good and evil, rather than a decadent, as some earlier critics had argued. Moreover, it is his innovative use of dramatic strategies – in this case, his employment of ritual and ceremony – which allow him to achieve his moralistic aim. The significance of this critical reading is, that like those of Bradbrook and Ekeblad, it aims to show that Webster's dramatic strategies – spectacular though they may be – are not simply sensationalist; rather, they serve a serious function, whether artistic or moral. So one of the main functions which twentieth-century criticism can be seen to possess is the re-evaluation of Webster's stagecraft: the examples above show how features and techniques of *The Duchess of Malfi* which had been taken by eighteenth- and nineteenth-century critics to be faults of the play, could be re-interpreted as aesthetic strengths.

Thus, John Russell Brown, in 1964, could praise 'the large and sweeping impression of the play in performance' (Hunter and Hunter 1969: 301), claiming that 'the simple eloquence of the shape of the action is especially impressive' (Hunter and Hunter 1969: 302), while A. W. Allison, in the same year, could write that 'the local and particular concerns of the play are subsumed into larger ethical configurations and at length form general statements of fitting dignity' (Hunter and Hunter 1969: 303). Such statements as these would have been all but unthinkable to most nineteenth-century readers of the play.

That said, the general move towards seeing Webster as a writer concerned with questions of morality, and of exploring the difference between good and evil, was not necessarily to lead to a more optimistic construction of the playwright's vision. For Ralph Berry, writing in 1972:

> *The Duchess of Malfi* does not postulate an ordered universe at all. It offers a vision of a meaningless universe, a context for humanity irretrievably prone to corruption and error, a situation in which the individual has no recourse but to generate his own values and to decide on his own course of action, futile though it may be. (Berry 1972: 107)

Berry is not a Kingsley or an Archer, hostile to Webster on moral or aesthetic grounds; quite the opposite, his book is an attempt to demonstrate the baroque artistic principles underlying Webster's drama. The pessimistic vision outlined by Berry is not judged as inaccurate or inadequate; but it does, perhaps, represent a challenge to those who view Webster as a moralist, at least as far as that term suggests that there is a good which can be achieved by human agents.

Even towards the end of the twentieth century, the fourth act of the play, and its relationship to the fifth act, still elicited significant comment from readers and critics. Jacqueline Pearson, in her study of the tragicomic elements in Webster's play, centred her discussion of *The Duchess of Malfi*, as many critics before her had also done, on the fourth act of the play: 'the fourth act of *The Duchess of Malfi*, then, presents a tragedy in which a good woman achieves a tragic self-assertion' (Pearson 1980: 88–9). Again formal concerns can clearly be seen to be in operation here: Pearson is concerned with the generic aspects of the play, particularly the relationship between tragedy and other dramatic forms; but she is also clearly working in a long critical tradition which views Act Four – the imprisonment, torment and death of the Duchess – as the emotional, moral, or aesthetic heart of the play. M. C. Bradbrook, returning to a study of the play in 1980, likewise found the formal qualities, and the influence of a variety of dramatic forms, to be one of the most significant features of the play: 'the play, from beginning to end, depends upon varying or enlarging, contracting or inverting the forms of a masque' (Bradbrook 1980: 161). So 'masque' can be added to 'tragicomedy', 'ceremony', and 'ritual' as non-tragic dramatic forms which twentieth-century critics have seen as informing the experimental dramatic structure of *The Duchess of Malfi*. In many ways, then, it is precisely Webster's departures from conventional dramatic structure – which, of course, earned him the censure of eighteenth-century critics and audiences – which have contributed most forcefully to the wholesale re-evaluation and canonisation of the dramatist over the course of the twentieth century.

RECENT READINGS

The most recent critical readings of *The Duchess of Malfi* are, in many respects, recognisably indebted to the critical discussions of the nineteenth and twentieth centuries: critics continue to discuss the nature of the supernatural in the play, for instance, or the likely audience response to the Duchess's sexuality. But they tend to do so from a rather different critical perspective, one that reads the play through the influence of a number of intellectual lenses, including feminism, Marxism, and other forms of literary theory. In general terms, criticism of *The Duchess*, like criticism of the English Renaissance in general, has become politicised: critics are interested in the relationship between the private and public spheres, in representations of male and female selves, sexualities and bodies, and, perhaps most pressingly, in questions of power, exploitation and injustice. The section that follows will outline some of the dominant concerns of contemporary critical discussion of the play, focusing on both the issues of individual identity raised by the play and on the text's engagement with wider social concerns of privacy and political authority.

Catholicism and the Demonic

That the play is concerned with 'horror' now seems neither as bizarre and tasteless as it did to many of the nineteenth-century critics, nor, perhaps as immediate and profound as it did to many critics writing in the wake of the second-world war; contemporary Western culture, of course, has sanitised torture and violence, repackaged it as entertainment, and, all too frequently, as *realpolitik*. Webster's taste for violence, to many twenty-first century readers, seems of a piece with that of many of his contemporaries, and the popular appeal of witnessing violence enacted is, unfortunately, one that requires no leap of cultural imagination from a twenty-first century perspective. Part of the effect of this is that critics no longer feel the need to explain away, or apologise for, Webster's interest in violence and the supernatural, and can concentrate on teasing out the wider cultural implications of Webster's particular techniques; this is true for the masque of madmen, the dead hand, the wax figures, the echo from the grave, and Ferdinand's lycanthropy; it is the latter which this section will examine by way of example.

Lycanthropy, as recent critics have shown (Hirsch 2005: 11), was a well-known affliction in early modern Europe, and could be considered in one of two ways: as an example of the intervention of supernatural (in this case demonic) agents in human affairs; or as what we might term a psychological disease, an affliction of the mind. In terms of the former interpretation, lycanthropy was considered as a sub-species of demonology and witchcraft, both of which, of course, had many fervent believers. It was, however, feared to a greater extent (and perhaps, believed in to a greater extent) in continental Europe than in England, perhaps due to the greater likelihood of being attacked by a (non were-)wolf on the continent (Hirsch 2005: 11).

From this perspective, of course, lycanthropy was considered as an evil in a grand cosmological scheme, which pitted the forces of Christianity against the forces of diabolism. Werewolves were like witches: they were threatening, non-human, forces willing to attack from outside the Christian community (Hirsch 2005: 29). They were also, in that sense, like members of non-Christian religions: Jews and Muslims were frequently demonised by early modern European Christians. Among the most threatening things about werewolves and non-Christians was the fact that they could not be visually distinguished from the normative Christian (caricatures of Jews and Muslims, of course, could be represented as either comically or threateningly different from the Christian community, and frequently were in both dramatic and written texts); the werewolf seems to be a human, until such time as he actually becomes a wolf. Similarly, intra-Christian tensions were couched in the same terms. In a Protestant society like Jacobean England, how could one be sure that one's neighbours weren't Catholics (and hence, according to popular fear and paranoia, likely to be engaged in treason or other nefarious plots)? The simple answer, of course, is that one couldn't, at least not by looking at them. A metaphorical equation between Catholics and wolves had been common in English writing since the earliest days of the Reformation. On one level, then, the transformation of Ferdinand from Catholic Duke to supernatural wolf reinforces many of the religious prejudices of Webster's audiences, particularly when Ferdinand is allied so closely with his brother the Cardinal, and hence with the political authority of the Catholic church. Brett D. Hirsch has convincingly argued that:

> For a Jacobean audience, the werewolf and the Catholic were similar beasts: both were essentially 'wolves dressed as men', otherwise indistinguishable from the rest of society but still a

threat to both church and state, and both as depraved, bloody, and ruthless as each other. (Hirsch 2005: 34)

Depraved, bloody, and ruthless, of course, is a fine description of Ferdinand's behaviour over the course of the play, and Webster's use of the werewolf image can thus be seen to have a clear strategic function in the drama: it draws on a link already present in early modern Protestant culture between wolves and Catholics, intensifying it to establish the evil nature of Ferdinand. Whether that evil is intended to be ultimately political or spiritual in nature is not clear, and may well depend on the particular prejudices of the individual audience member: but Webster does not seem to preclude either interpretation.

Gender Studies

If the discourses of lycanthropy and anti-Catholicism can be seen to serve very specific social functions in the early-seventeenth century, so too most current critics stress the social function of gender identities, the sense that masculinity and femininity are not solely determined by biology, but result from a complex process of interaction and negotiation with cultural pressures and ideals. This has proved a very fruitful way of analysing literary texts of the early modern period, particularly those, like *The Duchess of Malfi*, which appear to draw on a distinction between masculinity and femininity, and on appeals to the question of what is 'appropriate' behaviour for both men and women. On one level, the play can be seen as structured according to a sense of gender roles, with the duchess forming the female 'apex' of two male triangles, the aristocratic one of Ferdinand and the Cardinal, and the socially mobile one of Antonio and Bosola (Correll 2007: 90). In this reading of the play, the Duchess' identity as woman, and hence the very category of 'woman' itself, is defined in opposition to that of male identities; moreover, the Duchess is firmly located in, one might even say enclosed or trapped within, these structures of masculine relationships. As the main link between the aristocratic world and the less socially elevated world of Antonio and Bosola, the Duchess might even be seen as unwittingly reinforcing the structures of masculine power and dominance which restrict the influence of women in this society (an alternative view, of course, would be to look at the social mobility which has occurred at the end of the play – particularly the elevation of Antonio – and ascribe this to the Duchess's schematic position; the problems with this, of course, are firstly that the Duchess has had to die for this social change to come about, and secondly, that masculine authority is reasserted in the final outcome).

The central issue, in this way of reading the play, is how to respond to the world without the Duchess: has she pointed the way towards a better future, sacrificing herself in an almost messianic fashion in order to achieve that future? Or is she simply another victim of the masculine power struggles of Renaissance Italy (and, by implication, of Jacobean England)? For the critic Barbara Corell, the fall from power of the aristocrats after the Duchess's death reveals how important her social role in the world of the play always was:

> Without the living presence of the duchess between them, the male actors left in the opposing triangles are unmoored, affectively and socially; they proceed to fall, at times precipitously, from their positions. (Corell 2007: 91)

As a description of what 'happens', of course, this is entirely correct; but it doesn't give a reader or audience a sense of the correct response to the instability which the play presents.

If the Duchess is involved in relationships of subordination with her brothers, she is also, of course, a figure of some power and authority in her own right; here too the play seems to enact an exploration of gender identities, as political power is unconventionally located in a woman. Of course, it was not unknown for individual women to hold political power in early modern Europe; in England alone, the two monarchs who reigned prior to James were both female, resulting in a half-century of female rule. But these examples call attention to the differences between female and male rulers in the question of marriage: Mary Tudor's marriage to Philip of Spain was deeply unpopular, as the implicit gender dynamics of the match suggested to many English people that it was Philip who held power in the relationship. Elizabeth I, meanwhile, perhaps learning from the example of Mary, maintained power and authority largely as a result of staying unmarried. The position of the Duchess, of course, is different to both Mary (who married a figure of considerable international power) and Elizabeth (who did not marry): she wishes to marry a man considerably beneath her social station. This opens up a whole new series of political questions. As Sid Ray has argued:

> If wives were subject to husbands, then the ruling woman's new husband would become her head and thus, by extension, the head of the state. He would also become the head of the child ruler – in this case, the Duchess's son by the former duke – awaiting his majority. (Ray 2007: 22–3)

This was a problem which Elizabeth's subjects never had to deal with; but Elizabethan political theorists exercised themselves in working out the details of such a schema, in the event that it ever would come to pass. According to Ray, Webster (via the Duchess) outlines a very different way of dealing with the problem: 'by presenting an overtly female body as she rules the duchy, she calls into question the *de facto* masculinity of bodified representations of sovereignty' (Ray 2007: 23). There is a question, of course, as to how far the Duchess's body – explicitly female in its pregnancy and associated physiological reactions – is presented as a *successful* ruling body; as argued above, the body of the Duchess has to be physically disposed of before the new masculine hierarchy of Malfi can come into being. Ray's sense that the Duchess's female mode of government is 'based on [. . .] democratic principles of advice and consent [. . .] she preaches a philosophy of merit rather than inheritance' is by no means the only possible interpretation of what the play presents to us (Ray 2007: 23). The claim that 'Webster suggests that the female body is well-equipped for authority described as double-bodied, and thus he seems to naturalize and legitimize female rule' may be optimistic given the events of the play's second half (Ray 2007: 28).

What does seem clear is that the Duchess, as well as being presented as a figure of female authority, is also explicitly presented as a maternal figure, and her role as both pregnant woman and mother of children has generated some of the most intense critical debate of recent years. Part of the problem is how one is to conceptualise, historically speaking, the Duchess's role as mother of her family: she seems at times to speak to a bourgeois, modern, sense of the family unit which, historians tell us, would be anachronistic for the aristocratic families of the early seventeenth century. This point will be discussed in greater detail later, but it is worth drawing attention to it at this moment, as the respective role of men and women in the family appears to be a concern of the play, just as does the role of men and women in the state.

Of course, gendered identities are constructed and experienced in a variety of ways in early modern culture, much as they are in later cultures. Much critical attention has focused on the way in which Renaissance England understood and perceived the body, both in its gendered capacity (that is, as either male or female) and in the relationship between the body and the early modern sense of selfhood (for example, is individual identity felt to be related to the body, the 'soul' or 'mind', or some conjunction of the two?). The question has particularly concerned critics of Renaissance drama, as it is in the intense physical performativity of the drama that many of the culture's most insistent concerns on the nature of bodily identity can be seen to be played out; we have already seen, for example, the emphasis on the pregnant body of the Duchess throughout the play. What difference does it make, we might ask, that this pregnant body would have been represented on stage by a boy dressed as a woman? How far would this have altered the way in which the audience reacts and responds to the Duchess?

There are, of course, no easy answers to such questions, but asking them allows critics to begin to explore the preoccupations and concerns of Renaissance dramatists. Once the body is established as a site of enquiry for the play, it soon becomes apparent that bodies are a focus of attention in a variety of ways. Bosola, for example, in his role of malcontent is continually drawing attention to the perceived duplicity and falsehood of female bodies; and the play is full of images of disfigured or damaged bodies (the dead man's hand, for example). What Wendy Wall has referred to as 'the gross mortality of the putrefying body' is an important concern of the play too (Wall 2006: 169): a strain of rhetoric throughout the play suggests that bodies in their animated form are impure and corrupt, and the processes of decay and liquefaction after death are needed to 'purify' the rotten body.

Again, the apparently transformative body of Ferdinand is an important masculine context for the conventionally changeable feminine body. If the Renaissance masculine body is supposed to represent a constancy which contrasts with the fluidity of femininity, there is no sign of that in Webster's play. Rather, reading Ferdinand's lycanthropy as a fluidity of the sense of bodily identity presents an implicit challenge to that dichotomy. Hirsch's argument that early modern English demonologists became, over the course of the period, increasingly likely to see lycanthropy 'in wholly medical terms' is important here (Hirsch 2005: 8); Hirsch suggests that 'Ferdinand's lycanthropy is clearly treated in medical, natural terms, as are other instances of disease in the play' (Hirsch 2005: 17); that is, it is a disease of the body, rather than of the mind or the soul. Of course, if lycanthropy is, for these early moderns, a bodily disease, it is nevertheless a disease which interrogates the very nature of the body which it afflicts: it 'threatens the identity of being human and the precarious boundary between man and beast' (Hirsch 2005: 29). What Hirsch, like Wall, sees as Webster's insistent emphasis on the bodily, rather than supernatural, nature of disease in *The Duchess of Malfi* has important implications both for the vision of society outlined in the play – 'a medical universe with eschatological overtones, rather than vice versa' (Hirsch 2005: 43) – and for the assumed moral comment of the dramatist and, implicitly, the audience:

> The horror in *The Duchess of Malfi* comes, for the most part, from the knowledge that *real* people are capable of committing depraved acts; that intemperate anger and Machiavellian ambition can push a man past the limits of civility, and perhaps even past the border of the human. (Hirsch 2005: 43)

Thus the play's emphasis on the bodily nature of humanity, pushed to an extreme, results in an interrogation of the notions of both 'embodiment' and 'humanity'.

All of which, of course, suggests that the play is centrally concerned with the nature of selfhood: how do these characters define their individual identities, whether to themselves or to others, and how might this relate to the ways in which audience members conceptualise their own senses of selfhood? Garrett Sullivan's sense that the play dramatises 'complex relations among identity, subjectivity and agency' is a useful summary of the critical assumptions behind this way of reading the play (Sullivan 2005: 110). ('Subjectivity' in this sense is the 'consciousness of one's perceived states' or 'the quality or condition of viewing things exclusively through the medium of one's own mind or individuality' (OED); 'agency' refers to 'the power of a human subject to exert his or her will in the social world' (Castle 2007: 306).) In an original reading of the play, Sullivan suggests that the language of sleep reiterated throughout the play is central to the ways in which characters, particularly Ferdinand and the Duchess, experience and define their sense of self-identity: the Duchess 'is able to craft out of her brother's opprobrium both a desiring self and the space within which to execute her desires' (Sullivan 2005: 117), while Ferdinand is able to undertake a 'form of self-dispersal, the extension of the self across the bodies of those who perform actions for him' (Sullivan 2005: 117–18).

For Sullivan, sleep is doubly important in the play. Firstly, because sleep 'functions [. . .] to constitute a subject in terms of the disruption of his or her identity' (Sullivan 2005: 119) and, secondly, because:

one can also read the play's emphasis on sleep in terms of conscience as described in casuistical texts that proliferated in the late sixteenth and seventeenth centuries. Webster's play is saturated with references to conscience, and as we will see Ferdinand's madness marks not only the end of his sleep but the rousing of his dormant conscience. (Sullivan 2005: 119)

Thus Sullivan works, as most recent critics do, to establish a credible and convincing early modern context for the play; the critical aim is both to elucidate an unfamiliar historical context for a modern audience, and to demonstrate the significance of the play's intervention in ongoing debates. The early modern self, Sullivan and others imply, is experienced in quite different ways to the twenty-first-century self, and it is necessary for readers of Webster's play to be aware of some of these significant differences. The outcome of this is that Sullivan can claim that 'the Duchess's subjectivity emerges out of her resistance to the identity that her brothers attempt to craft for and impose on her' (Sullivan 2005: 125). He resists any suggestion that this is a simple or straightforward process, either in the manner of its operation in the play, or in the nature of the audience response: rather, the play describes 'modes of behaviour and forms of subjectivity that [. . .] do not easily lend themselves to a simplistic moral or ethical valuation' (Sullivan 2005: 130).

Sexuality

If sleep is central to the ways in which characters imagine their identity in the play, so too, and perhaps more intuitively, is sexuality. For Sullivan, sleep and sexuality are intimately linked: 'sleep connotes and enables sexual desire [. . .] the surrogate voyeurism of Ferdinand and the wilful sexual congress of the Duchess' (Sullivan 2005: 118). Many other recent critics, while not sharing Sullivan's interest in sleep and conscience, nevertheless make equally powerful claims for the centrality of sexuality as both a major preoccupation of the play, and an appropriate theoretical lens for critical reflection on it.

For Correll, for example, the Duchess's sexuality is less related to theological or moral matters such as conscience, and more related to her understanding of the world in the terms of the new economies emerging in the period: 'her candor, jarring to some of her critics, stems less from her use of sexual double entendres than from the language of the marketplace' (Correll 2007: 81). That is, she is a transitional figure who rejects the old world of the aristocracy (including the arranged marriages) and embraces the new world of an emergent bourgeois economy (including the right to choose one's own marital partner). For Wall, meanwhile, the Duchess is 'daringly and assertively' in control of her own sexuality

(Wall 2006: 159). What is more, 'knowing how to manage bodily processes becomes a key expressive motor of identification in the play' (Wall 2006: 165). It is not just Ferdinand and the Cardinal who wish to control the Duchess's body; she too needs to be in charge of her bodily desires and urges and, at least until the play's midpoint, appears to be more than capable of successfully carrying out such a task.

It is, of course, not just the Duchess's sexuality on which the audience is asked to comment; the supposition that Ferdinand is motivated by incestuous desire for his sister, whether unconscious or not, continues to be widely accepted by critics of this play. Moreover, it has been suggested that this 'unconventional' sexuality is apparent in Ferdinand's later descent into lycanthropy as well:

> Webster's werewolf also engages in contemporary anxieties about sexual identity, as Ferdinand's lycanthropy not only threatens his humanity, but his masculinity as well [. . .] While the boundary between masculine and feminine is already blurred by the aggressiveness of female sexuality in the play, Webster's representation of masculine sexuality, whittled away by melancholy, further interrogates these distinctions. (Hirsch 2005: 31)

So the play reveals anxieties not just about gender identities and the associated social roles, but also about the nature of sexual desire and the associated gendered forms of behaviour.

Of course, such anxieties as surround the body, selfhood, and sexuality are inextricably intertwined in early modern culture. The domain of sexuality is also, the play suggests, the world of the unencumbered self, what Sullivan refers to as 'a sphere of activity marked by the pursuit of desire and removed from [. . .] the world of public responsibility' (Sullivan 2005: 112); that is, something close to pure self-gratification, to the fulfilment of the Freudian *id* (that is, in the definition of the *OED*, 'the inherited instinctive impulses of the individual, forming part of the unconscious'). A psychoanalytic reading of the play might further stress Ferdinand's repression of his sexual desires – 'for most of the play Ferdinand is conspicuously absent from the Malfian court, relying on others to feed his voyeurism' (Sullivan 2005: 116) – as contributing to his later psychic disintegration.

Society

If the play offers us insights into the way in which Renaissance writers imagined the psychology of the individual, it also gives us some insight into the structures of society in this transitional moment in European history. As suggested earlier, one of the questions which critics ask of the play is to do with its place in narratives of the move towards modernity, in terms of the emergence of the nuclear family unit (which would, in this case, be the Duchess, Antonio, and their children, as opposed to the dynastic family unit from which the Duchess separates herself), and the emergence of a sharp divide between the private and public spheres. The issues are related, of course, as the family unit which the Duchess forges with Antonio is 'private' by necessity. But if the wider narrative of European history is that a separation between the public and private spheres happens gradually over the course of the early modern period, it is difficult to account for the apparently fully-formed nature of this division in a dramatic text from early seventeenth-century England. Wall has usefully summarised the critical dilemma of interpretation:

> The Duchess is said to use tragic maternalism to pit a newly affirmed family life in opposition to a sordid public life, a gesture alternately applauded as eroding the hierarchical character of the family, mourned as capitulation to a narrow definition of female agency and domesticity, or simply noted as registering contradictions in then current ideologies of gender. (Wall 2006: 150)

Wall's critical method is to analyse in detail the scene in which the Duchess, facing her death, gives orders for her children to be looked after; the result is a challenge to some of the conventional critical responses to the scene. For example, Wall claims that 'privacy makes no sense here as a synonym for domesticity, especially since the Duchess's idiosyncratic choice to make her family life covert can hardly be representative of any social formation of the family' (Wall 2006: 164). So the divide between the public and the private spheres is not what we are witnessing here, even though the Duchess 'does not bid farewell wondering about the public circulation of her story or the political fate of her realm' (Wall 2006: 166). What is more, the Duchess 'declines to die domestically' even as she accepts the necessity of her death (Wall 2006: 171). Wall's conclusion, simply stated, is that 'the play will not truly fit neatly into well-known stories about the rise of modernity' (Wall 2006: 169).

For all that, however, the play does give voice to a characteristically early modern concern about the changing nature of social allegiances, the rise of social mobility, and the threat to established hierarchical order. At a schematic level, the play traces a movement which could be argued to uncannily reflect the replacement of the aristocracy (Ferdinand and the Cardinal) with a new 'middle-class' power base (Antonio and his son). Such a schematic sketch is, of course, simplistic, and fails to take into account the diverse energies of the play; but a good deal of those energies are certainly directed towards interrogating the conventional structures of power and authority in Malfi.

This is a claim with which almost all recent critics of the play could agree. Correll, for example, is particularly interested in this aspect of the play, noting how Webster's foregrounding of the steward Antonio serves to highlight 'issues of social transition, service, class formation, and conflict' (Correll 2007: 65). It is significant, too, that Bosola shares a social position with Antonio, a 'steward' of sorts to Ferdinand. The gendered dynamics of the Duchess's relationships with Antonio and Bosola were discussed earlier; but the 'class' dynamics are equally as important:

Webster [. . .] strategically positions a strong aristocratic female character in relation to two steward figures, heightening class issues and more strongly foregrounding historically embedded concerns about power relations, gender, and class in a period of challenges to the feudal political structure. (Correll 2007: 69)

Subtly challenging Wall's conclusion that 'the play will not truly fit neatly into well-known stories about the rise of modernity' (Wall 2006: 169), Correll suggests that this lack of a 'neat fit' is one of the interests of the play; the Duchess 'combines elements of residual and emergent social formations [. . .] she occupies more than one historical location' (Correll 2007: 71). This means that those binaries of opposition – between the court and the marketplace, between the private and public spheres – which are employed in the conventional narrative of historical change are not separate in the play, but are nevertheless enmeshed and simultaneously present: 'the duchess uses the market in a destabilising way [. . .] by unmasking the already interdependent relation between market and court, as well as its place in the private sphere' (Correll 2007: 81). So, the destabilisation of conventional social models allows, for example, Antonio's social mobility (Correll 2007: 82). But of course, the simultaneous existence of two models of social inter-action creates a considerable degree of tension. On one hand, the Duchess demands recognition of her social status when she exclaims 'I am Duchess of Malfi still' ('she has hereditary rights, political responsibilities, and property' (Correll 2007: 83)); on the other hand, her elevation of Antonio threatens to negate the very basis of that aristocratic identity: 'the play acknowledges that a mediating figure like the estate steward does much to contaminate putative aristocratic purity' (Correll 2007: 83). Thus the Duchess is triangulated in both conventional aristocratic relationships (with Ferdinand and the Cardinal) and less familiar 'mixed-class' rela-tionships with Antonio and Bosola (Correll 2007: 85).

Other critics trace similar tensions in the plays. For example Ray's emphasis on examining the cultural significance of the Duchess's pregnant body allows him to claim that not only does Webster 'recast female authority as natural', but also that the play is able to 'subvert the underpinnings of absolutist discourse' (Ray 2007: 17). So there is an implicit challenge to the political aspect of the dominant social order as well. This critic goes on to suggest that the inheritance of the duchy by Antonio's son, rather than by the Duchess's son from her first marriage (as would be the 'correct' aristocratic procedure) is not, as many critics suppose, an oversight on Webster's part, but rather 'deliberate and meaningful', giving a specific social instance of the Duchess's 'belief that grafting betters nature' (Ray 2007: 24). The Duchess's authority, he claims, 'does indeed continue to exist' (Ray 2007: 26). This may be a slightly different, and perhaps more subtle, way of reading the play than Sullivan's suggestion that 'the Duchess is like Marlowe's Edward II or Shakespeare's Richard II in that she reveals greatest nobility of spirit once the trappings of her noble birth and rule have been stripped from her' (Sullivan 2005: 125), but the response of both critics suggests that the play is intensely engaged with pressing issues of social status and mobility. It is correct to claim, then, that contemporary criticism has begun to take the political tragedy of the play seriously; in doing so, it has moved critical discussion of the play away from the fourth act as an individual entity, and towards a focus on the play in its entirety.

CHAPTER 5

'Worthy Parts': *The Devil's Law-Case*

Although *The White Devil* and *The Duchess of Malfi* are Webster's most frequently read and performed works, nevertheless *The Devil's Law-Case* is increasingly coming to be seen as an important text in its own right. This chapter outlines some of the ways in which critics have engaged with this play, unique in Webster's oeuvre as a sole-authored tragicomedy.

ANALYSIS

The Devil's Law-Case has attracted much less critical attention than either *The White Devil* or *The Duchess of Malfi*, at least in part because the play does not easily sit alongside an image of Webster, common in both popular and academic writing, as primarily a tragic dramatist. Particularly in the centuries preceding the twentieth, commentary on *The Devil's Law-Case* seems to have been rare indeed. Webster himself, in the preface to the printed edition of the play, considered it as worthy of sharing the company of the two tragedies; addressing a potential patron, Sir Thomas Finch, Webster wrote:

> Some of my other works, as *The White Devil*, *The Duchess of Malfi*, *Guise* and others, you have formerly seen. I present this humbly to kiss your hands and to find your allowance. (Dedication, 4–7)

It is difficult to take the evaluation of the play's merits at face value here, as Webster is clearly aiming at securing some financial patronage from Finch. The play which Webster here refers to as *Guise* has been lost, but was almost certainly a tragedy based around the life of the French nobleman, the Duke of Guise; if that is the case, we can at least say that Webster perceived no contradiction in considering *The Devil's Law-Case* in conjunction with his tragedies of 'great men.'

The play's opening act has three main dramatic functions: to introduce the character of Romelio, arguably the play's central figure, and a development in some ways of the malcontent figures of Flamineo and Bosola; to introduce the nature of the relationship between Romelio and Contarino; and to introduce the relationship between Contarino and Leonora. The exposition of Romelio, a merchant, is carried out largely in his own words, although the audience does learn of his occupation and financial success through the expression of his interlocutor, Prospero: 'I did not think [that is, until now], / There had been a merchant lived in Italy / Of half your substance' (I, i, 1–3). Romelio's wealth is presented to the audience as exceptional, a fact of which he is clearly aware: 'Never in my life / Had I a loss at sea' (I, i, 10–11). Romelio's self-made mercantile wealth allows him, still in conversation with Prospero, to contrast himself with Contarino, a representative of the gentry: 'What tell you me of gentry? 'Tis nought else / But a superstitious relic of time past' (I, i, 33–4). Thus the play immediately engages with some of the 'social' concerns which also inform *The Duchess of Malfi* (see pp. 126–9). Such disdain, however, is not on display in the conversation which takes place between Contarino and Romelio, in which Contarino outlines his intention to marry Jolenta, the sister of Romelio. Although Romelio agrees to the match, Contarino, in soliloquy, outlines his distrust of the former's character: 'I do observe how this Romelio / Has very worthy parts, were they not blasted / By insolent vainglory' (I, i, 105–7). The audience's knowledge of Contarino's intentions towards Jolenta informs its understanding of the third movement of the scene, in which Contarino seeks the permission of Leonora (mother of Jolenta and Romelio) for the marriage, but in terms which are ambiguous and open to misinterpretation: 'I have a suit to you [. . .] 'Tis to bestow your picture on me' (I, i, 135–6). Contarino, again in soliloquy, reveals his confidence that Leonora has 'ingeniously perceived / That by her picture, which I begged of her, I meant that fair Jolenta' (I, i, 189–91). The audience is less convinced, and is therefore prepared for some of the erotic entanglements which will succeed.

The second scene develops the intricacies of the plot in two ways. The first is to introduce Ercole, a rival suitor for the marriage of Jolenta; the second is to allow Jolenta to inform Contarino of Ercole's pursuit, and therefore to prepare the audience for the conflicts of the succeeding acts. Ercole, a Knight of Malta, is clearly Romelio and Leonora's preferred choice for Jolenta's husband; the dramatic action of the scene consists largely of Romelio and Leonora's attempts to persuade Jolenta to accept Ercole's offers of marriage, and Jolenta's corresponding refusal. Ercole is presented to the audience as a noble character, unaware of any scheming on the part of the family. When Jolenta informs Contarino of her family's plans to ensure she marries Ercole, Contarino vows to take advantage of Ercole's enforced absence (he is due to go to sea 'For an expedition 'gainst the Turk' (I, ii, 80)): 'Tomorrow we'll / Be married' (I, ii, 259–60). The act ends with Contarino assuming all problems have been solved, but with his language – 'Let those that would oppose this union [. . .] entangle themselves / In their own work like spiders' (I, ii, 260–3) – suggesting to the audience the complex plots still to unfold.

An almost contemporary response to the play's plotting exists in the manuscript commonplace book of Abraham Wright (the same writer who also recorded his impressions of *The White Devil* and *The Duchess of Malfi*). As noted above, Wright was writing during the period of theatrical closure occasioned by the civil war, and so must almost certainly have encountered Webster's plays as printed documents. He is less impressed with this play than with Webster's preceding tragedies:

> But an indifferent play. The plot is intricate enough, but if rightly scanned will be found faulty by reason many passages do either not hang together, or if they do it so sillily that no man can perceive them likely to be ever done. (Hunter and Hunter 1969: 36)

Wright's withering description of the play as 'silly' has been echoed in the responses of many readers, who find the play lacking in the gravitas so much a feature of Webster's tragic plays. If this may indicate a general 'literary' prejudice in favour of tragedy over comedy or tragicomedy (Wright, of course, seems not to have witnessed these plays in the theatre), it is nevertheless significant that Wright actually judges the play on its own merits: Jacobean tragicomedy was notable for the complexity of the plots, the skill of dramatists like John Fletcher being judged by their ability to create a harmonious resolution of complex tensions and difficulties. Wright's response suggests that, for this seventeenth-century reader, the play fails in one of its main aims.

Act Two, Scene One, has two important functions: to introduce the sub-plot via the character of Crispiano, and to further the main plot by arranging an encounter between Contarino and Ercole, the rival suitors to Jolenta. The next scene stages the duel between Contarino and Ercole, which has taken place before any of the other characters can prevent it. Although the two are evenly matched, and wound each other, it is Ercole who suffers most, losing consciousness before Romelio and others can intervene to stop the duel. When the duel is stopped, Ercole is presumed dead, and Contarino presumed dying: 'both of them are lost; we come too late,' says Prospero (II, ii, 32). The bodies are removed to clear the stage before the next scene.

Act Two, Scene Three begins with a conversation between Romelio and Ariosto, a legal companion of Crispiano, regarding the loss of Romelio's ships; it soon becomes clear to the audience that the financial loss may well have a significant effect on Romelio's attitude to his profession and to his conduct. The next action of the scene is the relation to Romelio and Leonora, by a Capuchin monk and two bellmen (recalling, perhaps, the Capuchins of *The White Devil* and Bosola's role as bellman in *The Duchess of Malfi*) of the deaths of Contarino and Ercole. This forms a context for Romelio's 'meditation' on death (II, iii, 94), one of the passages of the play which most forcefully recalls the Webster of the tragedies: Romelio broods on 'graves and vaults', 'funerals', 'black raiment', 'rotten trees', 'the last act', 'gentle bones', 'sacrilege', 'monument[s]', 'charnel[s]', and 'the last day' (II, iii,

94–130). The tragic vocabulary here emphasises the way in which Webster is again self-consciously exploring the building-blocks of dramatic texts, albeit less radically than in *The White Devil* and *The Duchess of Malfi*. Also recalling *The White Devil*, the play moves to make Webster's favoured dramatic set-piece of a trial now a very real possibility. The scene then ends on a final couplet which is also characteristic of the dramatist in its imagery and tone: 'So sails with fore-winds stretched do soonest break / And pyramids a'th'top are still most weak' (II, iii, 169–70).

Romelio recalls the malcontents of the tragedies again in Act Three, Scene Two, wherein Webster allows him to more fully develop his role as stage villain, as he enters dressed as a Jew (a stage convention for a scheming and manipulative villain in early modern England; Marlowe's Barabas in *The Jew of Malta*, for example, is an important precursor of Romelio's disguise). As disguise in *The Duchess of Malfi* was used to interrogate the very nature of selfhood (see pp. 102–3), so *The Devil's Law-Case* often suggests that there is little psychological substance beneath the performance of social identities.

Act Three, Scene Three begins with a tableau again reminiscent of Webster's earlier tragedies: '*A table [is] set forth with two tapers, a death's head, a book. [Enter] Jolenta in mourning, Romelio sits by her*' (III, iii, oSD). Mourning the death of Contarino, Jolenta is approached by Romelio to play a part in his unfolding plan: if she will pretend to be pregnant by Ercole, not only will she inherit Ercole's land, but Romelio will be able to secure an upbringing for the child which he has fathered upon a nun. Jolenta, of course, refuses, at which point Romelio fabricates a tale about Contarino's supposed lust for Leonora (the irony, of course, is that the audience has seen many hints of Leonora's lust for Contarino). Not only does this poison the memory of Contarino for Jolenta, it also allows Romelio to drive a wedge between mother and daughter: Jolenta then apparently agrees to Romelio's plan. Romelio relates Jolenta's supposed pregnancy to Leonora, who is much more concerned with the apparent death of Contarino; alone on stage, she reveals in soliloquy her desire for the latter. Upon the entrance of the Capuchin with Ercole (about to be revealed as alive), Leonora, distracted, inadvertently reveals Romelio's role in contributing to

Contarino's (apparent) death; Ercole notes this for future use. The Act ends with Leonora forming a plot with Winifred, a waiting-woman, to launch a law-suit (the 'devil's law-case' of the title, inevitably recalling 'The Arraignment of Vittoria') which will allow her to take her revenge on her son.

The tone of the play is at this point close to tragedy, and indeed there is some evidence that at least one early reader thought of the play in these generic terms. At around the same time that Abraham Wright was jotting down his responses to the plays in his common-place book, Samuel Sheppard was composing a poem, *The Fairy King*, which referred to Webster. Like Wright's work, Sheppard's poem is a handwritten manuscript, and appears not to have been printed for circulation. Of particular interest for a discussion of *The Devil's Law-Case* is the fact that Sheppard refers to Webster's 'three noble tragedies'. It is possible, of course, that Sheppard is here referring to *Guise* as the third of the tragedies, after *The White Devil* and *The Duchess of Malfi*. But, as Sheppard was born around the middle of the 1620s (King 2004), he would have been in his late teens when the theatres were closed in 1642; as such, it is unlikely that he would have witnessed all of Webster's plays in perform-ance. It is possible, then, that the third 'tragedy' he is referring to is *The Devil's Law-Case*; as all three of these plays had been printed, Sheppard, like Wright, may well have known Webster's works primarily as literary documents. Of course, this is specula-tive; if he had indeed read *The Devil's Law-Case*, Sheppard would have come across Webster's dedication, with its mention of the trio of tragedies; there would seem to be, then, no way of definitively ascertaining which play Sheppard is referring to at this point.

In any case, just as the dramatic centre of *The White Devil* was 'The Arraignment of Vittoria', so too Webster makes Act Four, Scene Two the dramatic centre of this play by staging a trial scene. And just as the earlier play began its trial scene with a dramatisation of the preparations on the edge of the trial itself, so too Webster employs that technique again in *The Devil's Law-Case*. The scene begins, then, with the entrance of Ercole, who arranges a seating position where he cannot be generally seen (contrasting with the visibility of Bracciano's entrance in *The White Devil*); thus, for most of the trial, he will serve as an observer, unwilling yet to fully reveal the fact of his survival. The next characters to enter are Contarino and the two surgeons who had been tending him as he lay (apparently) dying; all three are in disguise and, like Ercole, adopt a position on stage which gives them a good view of the proceedings (thus building on *The Duchess of Malfi*'s interest in commentary and observation). As the trial is Webster's main set-piece in this play, he carefully builds up to the central accusation levelled against Romelio. It emerges that Leonora is accusing Romelio of bastardy, hence accusing herself of adultery (her husband, of course, is no longer alive to be shamed by the accusation): 'this gentleman was begot / In his supposèd father's absence' (IV, ii, 230–1). Crispiano, as judge, is surprised that Leonora should confess to a crime which would seem to shame her, and suspects that there is a deeper motive for the mother's suit against the son. Pushing the enquiries further, he realises that he himself is accused of being the natural father to Romelio; revealing himself to the crowd gathered at the trial – 'I am the party that here stands accused / For adultery with this woman' (IV, ii, 471–2) – and making clear that he was in the East Indies in 1571, the year of Romelio's begetting, Crispiano ensures that Leonora's story is publicly revealed as the fabrication that it is. Escaping one accusation, Romelio nevertheless faces another as Ercole, revealing himself, accuses him of the murder of Contarino; as there is no evidence for the accusation, Ariosto (who has taken the place of judge because of Crispiano's involvement in the case) orders that a duel must take place. Contarino volunteers to stand for Ercole, though he has not yet revealed his true identity. Thus the anticipated climax of the trial ends, only to be replaced by another dramatic movement towards climax, as the act ends with the spectre of a duel to come. In this, Webster deliberately uses a very different dramatic structure to the tragic climax, followed by a post-tragic trauma, of *The Duchess of Malfi*.

Act Five, in contrast to the act immediately preceding, consists of a series of short scenes. It builds towards scene six, which stages the duel, which is interrupted by the entrance of Leonora and the Capuchin (Romelio, fearing the possibility of his death, gives orders for the two to be released immediately before the duel commences). The duel is stopped, Contarino is revealed as alive, and he vows his life to Leonora. Angiolella and Jolenta enter; the latter is also dressed as a nun. With all the main characters now alive and reconciled, the task of doling out rewards and punishments falls to the figure of Ariosto, who maintains his role as the play's voice of conscience and moral behaviour. His final speech, which is also the final speech of the play, draws the plot to a close, rewards the virtuous, and punishes the guilty: the play, as befitting its tragicomic generic status, closes on a note of harmonious reconciliation.

CURRENT CRITICAL RESPONSES

Economics

It is not until the late decades of the twentieth century that critics have begun to take *The Devil's Law-Case* seriously, and to discuss it alongside the tragedies as an example of Webster's intense dramatic vision. Over the past few decades, a critical interest in the play has become more common, and there is now a critical tradition of sorts regarding the play, something which could not be said before the middle of the twentieth century. Ralph Berry's influential book-length study of Webster, for example, devoted a chapter to *The Devil's Law-Case*, acutely observing that 'Romelio, Leonora, Contarino, and the rest are representatives of a society whose struggle for money and social status is observed with a bleak and unforgiving eye' (Berry 1972: 153). For Berry, the play is clearly engaged in commenting on the economic materialism of early seventeenth-century London, and as such should be seen as a satire in the mould of Jonson's or Middleton's city comedies, scathing commentaries on the economic preoccupations of early modern Londoners. Berry does not wish to fully reinvigorate the play's reputation – 'it may perhaps be conceded that Webster has not wholly succeeded in his enterprise' (Berry 1972: 153) – but the faint praise with which he discusses the play's ending – 'the existence of an ambiguity, a certain undischarged tension, at the final curtain is no infallible criterion of blame' (Berry 1972: 153) – does at least indicate that the critic perceives some measure of artistic success.

Genre and Gender

A chapter devoted to the play also appeared in Jacqueline Pearson's book-length study of the plays of Webster; as this critic's professed subject is 'tragicomic elements in Webster's plays' (Pearson 1980: 3), the importance accorded *The Devil's Law-Case* here should come as no real surprise. In accordance with her view of the tragedies as containing significant tragicomic elements, Pearson stresses the similarities between *The Devil's Law-Case* and Webster's earlier sole-authored plays: 'its world is recognisably the world of the tragedies only slightly modified' (Pearson 1980: 96). This is not, though, an attempt to ennoble the play by considering it as a tragedy; rather, Pearson is much more accommodating of the genre of tragicomedy than many earlier critics had been, thus negating the need to excuse or apologise for Webster's employment of the popular generic form. Although Pearson, like Berry, stresses the play's engagement in the concerns of its own time (referring to a 'dense field of contemporary reference' (Pearson 1980: 96)), she nevertheless takes greater steps towards a full rehabilitation of the play by arguing that it 'create[s] a world recognisably like our own' (Pearson 1980: 96). Thus the play, for Pearson, demands critical attention as urgently as do *The White Devil* and *The Duchess of Malfi*.

Lee Bliss, too, devoted a chapter of a book-length study of Webster to *The Devil's Law-Case*, but revealed a sense of disappointment: 'Despite flashes of greatness, *The Devil's Law-Case* is not a felicitous successor to Webster's tragedies' (Bliss 1983: 171). Thus the increased level of attention which the play had received was not enough to elevate it to a position in the canon alongside *The White Devil* and *The Devil's Law-Case*; yet Bliss still saw much of interest in the play, identifying it as another example, like the tragedies, of Webster's 'characteristic perspectivism, his penchant for opposing generic as well as thematic structures' (Bliss 1983: 171). The play, then, is characteristically Websterian in its juxtapositions of tone and genre – its aesthetic relativism, in other words – and the exploration of the tension between 'pragmatic materialism and romantic idealism' is of a piece with the preoccupations of the two tragedies (Bliss 1983: 172); like Pearson, Bliss is also aware that the tragedies possess generic hybridities all of their own, and are much less 'pure' than some of the nineteenth-century critics may have wished.

Although there have been few book-length scholarly studies of Webster's work in the last two decades, nevertheless the number of articles and essays discussing the play continues to grow, and the development of a critical tradition of interpreting the play does seem belatedly to be under way. The play's most recent editors are indebted to Bliss's work of the early 1980s, arguing that 'in certain respects Bliss's category of ironic tragedy seems to fit the Websterian bill' (Webster 2003: 33), but they also pay attention to the feminist criticism that has inspired much recent discussion of Webster and other Renaissance dramatists (see p. 73). Focusing on Webster's characterisation of Leonora, they claim that 'he confounds [. . .] the stereotypical representation of an ageing widow [. . .] Webster invests Leonora with a degree of sympathy which is remarkable' (Webster 2003: 33). Furthermore, arguing that '*The Devil's Law-Case* defies both expectation and categorization,' they make a claim that, until recently, most critics would have considered unthinkable: 'it proves itself a worthy descendant of *The White Devil* and *The Duchess of Malfi*' (Webster 2003: 33). The critical rehabilitation of *The Devil's Law-Case*, then, is far from complete, but is at least undoubtedly underway.

CHAPTER 6

'Gleefully Savage': The Tragedies in Performance

Webster's aesthetic relativism, radical and dramatically effective though it may be, presents challenges not just for critics aiming to discuss the nature of Webster's thought – whether aesthetic, moral, or political – but also for modern theatrical directors and producers, who face the difficult task of deciding how far to let Webster's aesthetic relativism have free rein or, alternatively, how far to impose a coherent aesthetic vision onto the relativism of the text. In the event, many of the most successful productions of Webster's plays have been attuned to the destabilising tendencies of Webster's dramatic strategies. It has also been the case that, in grappling with these issues, recent directors have called attention to aspects of the text which have also been of concern to literary critics. This chapter cannot engage with all of the important productions of Webster's tragedies. Its aim, therefore, is to focus on four significant late twentieth-century productions – two of *The White Devil* and two of *The Duchess of Malfi* – to suggest some of the fruitful ways in which actors and directors have approached Webster's texts.

DECADENCE AND EXTRAVAGANCE: *THE WHITE DEVIL*, NATIONAL THEATRE, 1969

All theatre productions, of course, are a creation of their own historical moment. Different times and different places re-create the drama of the past in their own image. Nowhere, perhaps, in the stage history of *The White Devil* is this more apparent than in the 1969 National Theatre, London, production, directed by Frank Dunlop and starring Geraldine McEwan as Vittoria. This was a production which imagined Webster's Renaissance Italy as a version of 1960s London, complete with all of the decadence, glamour, and extravagance of that period in the city's history; complete, too, with the fashions of the era, Vittoria's Act Five costume not a white gown but 'thigh-high white boots and [a] transparent lace mini-smock' (Webster 1995: 110). Most reviewers of the time were impressed by its stress on the relevance of Webster's play, but at least one thought that the production was 'continually balanced on the edge of caricature' (Wardle 1969: 8).

This was not, however, a production which uncritically brought contemporary fashion from the street to the stage. Rather, Frank Dunlop enlisted the assistance of the Italian set and costume designer, Piero Gherardi, to make the design of the production as central to the audience's engagement as were the actors' interpretations of their characters. Gherardi was most famous for his work with the iconic film director Federico Fellini, for whom he had designed *La Dolce Vita* and *8½*. This was, then, a Webster which promised to be in tune with the zeitgeist; in its emphasis on the design of a world rather than the interpretation of character as the primary task of a production, it is also emblematic of a significant strand of Websterian adaptation of the late-twentieth century (see pp. 147–50). Gherardi's input was central to the production's design and effect: he 'set the play in a blaze of light', with a backdrop of 'moving granite blocks which might have been stolen from Stonehenge' (Barber 1969). The granite blocks, which one critic likened to 'a monumental façade of huge, sun-baked boulders' (Marcus 1969), emphasised the insignificance of the characters, more than one reviewer likening them to 'insects' (Marcus 1969; Bryden 1969). This distinctive visual style was matched by nightmarish music (Barber 1969), and a flamboyantly theatrical approach to costuming, the actors 'overdressed' (Barber 1969) in 'cornucopian arabesques of lace' (Wardle 1969: 8), all in all representing 'a pageant of flamboyant corruption' (Bryden 1969). There were some predictably anti-spectacular responses to this bravura display – 'set and costumes have usurped the actors' task of comment and interpretation' (Bryden 1969) – but most critics were swept away by the 'perverted sensuality' which the 'immensely stylish production' brought 'into the open' (Marcus 1969).

Geraldine McEwan's portrayal of Vittoria, however, drew mixed responses from reviewers. The critic for the London *Daily Telegraph* was impressed with McEwan's performance, which was deemed inseparable from the influence of Gherardi's design:

> Dominating the whirlwind from the moment of her long first solo-walk across the stage is Virginia [sic] McEwan as Vittoria, her frail body and naked back enveloped by a cobra-hood, her face evil with the mixed satiety and appetite, leer and snigger, coquetry and indecency, of the consummate whore. Under a huge wig of candy-floss, her pretty vicious little head fascinates, while her always-odd voice, twanging like a false cello, uses words like whips and sentences like scorpions. Towards the end of the play, dressed now as a corrupt Peter Pan in thigh-high white boots and transparent lace, Miss McEwan dies chained to a rock, expiring with a death-rattle of the whole body, as if life were loath to leave a creature so rapacious. (Barber 1969)

Of course, the decision to allow Vittoria to dominate the play in this manner is a choice which influences the possibilities open to a production, and it negates a potential reading of the play which sees Vittoria as primarily a victim of the masculine power struggles of Renaissance Italy. The snake-like evil of Vittoria as a 'consummate whore' has the effect of reducing the conscious ambiguity which Webster strives for her in his portrait of Vittoria (perhaps *portraits* since, as noted above (p. 74), the play presents a series of radically disjunctive visions of the character). As David Carnegie suggests, this production ignored even the deliberate paradox of the play's title: 'no longer did either stage audience or theatre audience see a vision of a seeming innocent, a white devil with a fair exterior, nor of a real victim of a dark and oppressive system' (Webster 1995: 111). In some ways, then, Dunlop, Gherardi, and

McEwan's presentation of Vittoria is quite distinct from the vision presented by Webster's text.[1]

If there was a sense among audiences, then, that this was a Vittoria of the moment, removed from the Vittoria of 1612, the same feeling could be said to condition responses to the play as a whole. Many critics strove to identify the ways in which this production was not 'true' to what the reviewers considered to be the most appropriate ways of thinking about Webster: '[the production] removes Webster from the shadows and places him in the glaring sunshine' (Wardle 1969); 'Right or wrong, Webster's world is a consistent creation: here it is exploited to reveal a brutal exhibition of high camp' (Wardle 1969); 'Dunlop's production [. . .] cut sententiae and ethical statements such as Giovanni's final speech' (Webster 1995: 111). One reviewer even saw the production as being (correctly, in his view) rather hostile to the idea that the play was a work of significant dramatic merit: '[the production's] underlying attitude of the play seems to be that the poetry is immortal, the intrigue hopelessly over-complicated, the view of life adolescent' (Wardle 1969). Although Dunlop emphasised, in his programme notes, his sense that the play could speak directly to contemporary concerns – 'there is a scepticism about position, worldly glory, and people's outward behaviour that we recognise and feel deeply' (Dunlop 1969) – nevertheless most reviewers persisted with an idea of Webster which could have been derived almost directly from the Victorian critics. Even those reviewers who were impressed by the production shared this vision of Webster: '[the production presents] a hellish kind of place where the endless skulduggery, violence, luxuries, and lusts of John Webster's diseased imagination might conceivably have happened' (Barber 1969). Perhaps surprisingly, only the critic for the conservative *Sunday Telegraph* (although repeating the reductive vision of Webster) seemed to appreciate the counter-cultural energies being released in the production:

What sex is to us, death was to the Jacobeans. Of all the dramatists of this period, Webster was the supreme pornographer [. . .] He fairly drools over it, as he records lovingly each spasm and each intoxicating drop of blood. It ends in an orgy.

Flamineo, Vittoria, and her Moorish servant are strapped to the wall and slowly, protractedly, disembowelled. It is an erotic consummation for the killed as well as for the killers: an orgasmic union that leaves three exhausted and three dead. (Marcus 1969)

Here one gets some sense of the potential political work which this spectacular production was undertaking; its exploration of gender roles – and particularly of the power and social significance of sexual desire – was part of a wider cultural movement of the late 1960s. Critics have often been aware of how theatre directors often use the plays of Shakespeare to make (deliberately anachronistic) political statements; Dunlop and Gherardi were surely undertaking something similar with *The White Devil* in this production.

COURTLY CLAUSTROPHOBIA: *THE DUCHESS OF MALFI*, ROYAL EXCHANGE, MANCHESTER, 1980

If Dunlop's 1969 *White Devil* emphasised the glamour and spectacle of socially disruptive sexuality, then Adrian Noble's 1980 *Duchess of Malfi* – performed at the Manchester Royal Exchange, with Bob Hoskins as Bosola and Helen Mirren as the Duchess – emphasised the more repressive side of that equation, enlarging on the play's preoccupations with claustrophobia and confinement to present a pessimistically political tragedy. The Manchester Royal Exchange is a theatre in the round, where the audience surround the stage on all sides; Noble used the physical properties of the theatre to striking effect in this production. In contrast to the physical spectacle of Dunlop's *White Devil*, Noble employed a deliberate scarcity of physical resources, the first half of the play making use of 'a long strip of dazzling white lambswool carpet leading to a throne' and 'Monteverdi-like fanfares' to evoke the atmosphere of the ducal palace (Wardle 1980). Noble's approach to set design was widely praised:

> [. . .] he has mastered [the Royal Exchange's] resources. Not only in his use of the outer perimeter to carry the sounds from

the outer world (beautifully employed in the echo scene), but in projecting the open and secret elements of the play through frozen tableaux, decisive alternations of full light and spotlit gloom, and the substitution for the white carpet of a long blood-stained rag leading to a prison chair. (Wardle 1980)

As other critics have noted, this 'prison chair' was 'horribly evocative of an electric chair' (McCluskie and Uglow 1989: 55), the design thus calling attention to the play's preoccupations with justice and mercy (or, indeed, the lack of such qualities in Malfi).

The production, then, imagined the court of Malfi as a recognisably modern and realistic torture-chamber, not a house of horrors so much as the inquisitorial tool-house of a dictatorial regime. This was the case throughout the production, for example in the staging of the wax bodies ('no crude show of waxworks but real dead bodies rapidly wheeled in on operating tables' (McLuskie and Uglow 1989: 57)), the masque of the madmen ('terrifying grotesques [. . .] wheeled on in an enormous cage from which they were let out like savage animals' (McLuskie and Uglow 1989: 57)), and the 'horribly realistic dead man's hand' (McLuskie and Uglow 1989: 151). The production style as a whole was aptly characterised as 'a horrid mixture of Elizabethan barbarity and modern realism' (McLuskie and Uglow 1989: 159), the implication, of course, being that such barbarity is as modern as the realism.

This uncompromising directorial eye on the horrors of the play was by and large continued in the approaches of the actors. The acting was praised as 'a tough, extrovert reading' (Wardle 1980) and as 'brilliantly expansive' (McLuskie and Uglow 1989: 55). Most obvious, perhaps, was the way in which the actors and directors managed to make the play, often characterised as an absurd gothic melodrama, intensely *realistic*: 'the sight of these three [that is, Ferdinand, Julia, and the Cardinal] in the last scene, giggling with exhaustion and alternately hugging each other and delivering death strokes, is for once painfully credible' (Wardle 1980). Mike Gwilym's portrayal of Ferdinand was especially impressive, 'constantly pacing like the animal he was to become' (McLuskie and Uglow 1989: 56), 'capricious in his laughter, sinister in his quiet madness' (Webster 1995: 438).

The most divisive aspect of the production, perhaps, was Bob Hoskins' performance as Bosola. At this point in his career, Hoskins was yet to make the move into mainstream American films which occurred later in the decade, but he was a seasoned television performer, and his breakthrough British movie, *The Long Good Friday*, was released in the same year as this performance as Bosola. In some ways, Hoskins played Bosola in the style for which he would later become famous on screen, as 'a Cockney bravo, joking at death and achieving a rough comic flair' (Webster 1995: 438). By and large, this 'brusque approach' to Bosola was welcomed by critics (Wardle 1980): he 'look[ed] as if he [was] straight off the galleys' (Wardle 1980), he was 'as energetic in seizing comic changes [. . .] as in rising to the conscience-stricken poetry' (Wardle 1980), and:

> His rasping cockney accent emphasised the class difference between him and the Cardinal in their first encounter, but it also cut through the complex metaphors of his language to make his epigrams seem like the cleverest but most natural of remarks. (McLuskie and Uglow 1989: 56)

Although praise for Hoskins' approach to the role was widespread, and certainly seemed to fit with the directorial vision of the text, nevertheless it was not universal: 'he never found the malcontent, the scholar, or the moral ambiguity of the character' (Webster 1995: 438). Indeed, this production was of particular interest because it did not stress the ambiguity and relativism of Webster's text, yet still managed to present a successful interpretation, relevant to its audience.

Just as Hoskins was combining *The Long Good Friday* with *The Duchess of Malfi*, so too was Helen Mirren, who played the Duchess as a 'woman of knowing sexuality' (McLuskie and Uglow 1989: 57). Mirren's Duchess was clearly an aristocrat to Hoskins's cockney Bosola; and Mirren's approach to the character was not to present a portrait of passive stoicism, but rather to present the Duchess as an intensely emotional woman: the *Times* reviewer was struck by the 'vivid emotional detail' displayed (Wardle 1980). If Mirren's Duchess was as emotionally, physically, and sexually alive as Geraldine McEwan's 1969 Vittoria, nevertheless she struck audiences as both more realistic and more sympathetic than McEwan's character:

> She was lavishly and sexily dressed, and she too played up the comedy in the wooing scene. There was nothing pious in her passion for Antonio and the coy trick of the wedding ring invited and got uproarious laughter from the audience [. . .] But she was no stereotyped tart. She had an immense aristocratic dignity in the court scenes and seemed a woman who tried and almost succeeded in making her own world. (McLuskie and Uglow 1989: 57)

Mirren's Duchess, indeed, has been one of the most widely praised interpretations of the character in recent years, just as Noble's vision of the play has also been one of the most critically successful. The Duchess has been seen, in this production, to represent 'love and domesticity' against the torturous world of the brothers (Webster 1995: 438), and Mirren's presentation of her as a 'delicate, graceful, self-aware, but recklessly sexual' woman has impressed many (Webster 1995: 438).

DESIGNING DEATH: *THE DUCHESS OF MALFI*, NATIONAL THEATRE, 1985

If Adrian Noble's set design at the Manchester Royal Exchange in 1980 liberated his actors to explore the complexities of Webster's characterisation, most critics agreed that the opposite was the case for Philip Prowse's production of *The Duchess of Malfi* at the National Theatre, London in 1985. Prowse had directed Webster previously and had a track record of emphasising set and costume design over the performances of his cast. If this suggests that the production would be more like Dunlop and Gherardi's 1969 *White Devil* than Noble's 1980 *Duchess of Malfi*, nevertheless most critics felt that Prowse's production lacked the energy, urgency, and originality of Dunlop and Gherardi. Eleanor Bron's performance as the Duchess was not well received. The reviewer for *The Times* certainly was impressed visually with Bron, but was less impressed with her theatrical performance:

> From her first entrance, orientally veiled and inching towards us with infinite slowness, Eleanor Bron weaves a seductive web for the audience as well as for the unfortunate Antonio. It is as a kind of pre-Raphaelite beauty that she is most effective; however once she lets her hair down and starts discovering virtue through suffering, disbelief remains suspended. I hope she will grow into this role, if only because she looks so ravishing, but I believe she has yet to feel her way fully down the fatal path. (Cropper 1985: 9)

In many ways, this kind of reaction can be seen as the critical response to the production in miniature: captivating and arresting visually, but lacking in dramatic substance. Some critics explicitly blamed Prowse's design for the difficulties which the actors evidently had with the material (McLuskie and Uglow 1989: 62), while others noted that Bron lacked 'both early radiance and later tragic structure' and 'played Act IV with little emotion' (Webster 1995: 440). The contrast with the reception afforded Mirren just five years earlier could hardly be more stark.

Other actors were deemed to be more successful with their roles, even if critical response could hardly be said to have been overly enthusiastic. Just as 1980's Bosola was later to make a move into the cinematic mainstream, so too in the 1985 production Bosola was played by Ian McKellen. McKellen's training and background, however, were very different to that of Hoskins, and his theatrical experience informed his interpretation of Bosola, who he played in a much more nuanced manner than did Hoskins. If Hoskins emphasised the comedic aspects of Bosola's role, McKellen deliberately sought to de-emphasise such features:

> He played a mordantly cynical, diseased intellectual, doggedly loyal to his masters, and amiable to the audience (if not seizing the black humour of the part), and his scruffy costume, shorn hair, and scholar's glasses put him outside the decadent world of the grandees. (Webster 1995: 440)

A sense that McKellen brought 'exactly the right note of dogged integrity to the proceedings' was widespread (Cropper 1985: 9), even if some critics thought that his performance should be considered alongside that of Bron, as evidence that the play had been 'managed and manipulated beyond [. . .] recovery' (McLuskie and Uglow 1989: 62).

The manager-manipulator-in-chief was, of course, director-designer Philip Prowse, and Prowse's design was undoubtedly the star of the show, much more so than either Bron or McKellen. Indeed, the latter's effectiveness was at least in part a function of costume:

> There is an immediate and satisfying contrast between the well oiled, sometimes grotesquely stylized, attitudes of the courtiers in their filigreed finery and feathered hats, and the dowdy, slightly ungainly presence of Ian McKellen's malcontent. (Cropper 1985: 9)

Yet Prowse's characteristic directorial touches were more spectacular; thus, audiences were presented with 'the mute, cowled figure of Death which forms a silent commentary on the action by its constant presence' (Cropper 1985: 9), and with 'the abstract sound effects of clicking and knocking and unlocated mad crying' (McLuskie and Uglow 1989: 61). The problem with all this, for most critics, is that the atmospheric trappings did not connect with the audience's experience of the characters' dilemmas: 'Death [. . .] appeared more part of the setting of counter-reformation gloom than a portentous foreshadowing of all the character's fates' (McLuskie and Uglow 1989: 61).

This was a production, then, which saw Webster as did the Victorians, as a poet of 'relentless horror' (McLuskie and Uglow 1989: 61):

> These figures had no daytime existence and the lighting, often filtered through a grating above the stage, made the action seem to take place in a dungeon or at the bottom of a well. Lighting was also used to create enormous shadows which gave a depth and colour to the mainly black and white

design but which also emphasised the action's weighty and sinister feel. (McLuskie and Uglow 1989: 61)

Of course, this is a valid, if potentially derivative, directorial response to the text; but whereas Noble combined a distinctive design with an emphasis on sympathetic performances from the cast, Prowse – most reviewers felt – did not. Thus, 'the production seemed full of [. . .] embedded references which did not combine into a frame of meaning but vaguely grasped at a significance behind the story' (McLuskie and Uglow 1989: 61). One critic went so far as to say that 'Prowse was much possessed by death, much more than Webster' (Webster 1995: 440). This is not to say that the production was not praised; on the contrary, Prowse's production design did receive lavish praise in many quarters. The general sense, however, was that the design achieved a striking visual and atmospheric effect at the expense of the actors and their performances.

STAGING SEXUALITY: *THE WHITE DEVIL*, ROYAL SHAKESPEARE COMPANY, 1996

If Adrian Noble's 1980 production of *The Duchess of Malfi* has been the most enthusiastically received version of Webster's second tragedy in recent years, then the most successful recent production of *The White Devil* has almost certainly been that of the Royal Shakespeare Company in 1996, directed by Gale Edwards. Like Dunlop's production of 1969, this was a version of *The White Devil* intended resolutely for its contemporary audience; unlike Dunlop and Gherardi, however, Edward's production also aimed to present a recognisably Websterian vision of the play, thus suggesting that Webster's play remained relevant and resonant to an audience of the mid-1990s. The enthusiastic critical response suggests that the strategy was highly successful.

If audiences in 1980 responded well to Adrian Noble's relative restraint in his staging of *The Duchess of Malfi*, it was by contrast the excessive nature of the sex and violence in Edwards's *White Devil* which impressed reviewers and critics. A number of reviewers repeated an anecdote from the press performance in an attempt to capture the visceral, affective qualities of this production:

> So effective was the accumulation of poisonings, stabbings, shootings, and garottings at Thursday's matinee that a school-girl on the front banquette of the warm, wooden quasi-Eliz-abethan interior, fainted during the last act, banged her head on the front of the apron stage and revived a few minutes later only to see that the carnage was still in full flow. (Coveney 1996: 13)[2]

This is a Webster, then, of spectacular and excessive violence – of 'carnage' – and it seems unarguable that an interest in violent spectacle is an authentically Websterian concern. The same reviewer praised 'Webster's wonderful, hermetic world of vice, metaphor and chain reaction [which] takes us to the heart of darkness and corruption' (Coveney 1996: 13). What was most impressive about this production, then, was that – like Noble's *Duchess* – it offered access to the Websterian 'heart of darkness' without resorting to the conventional vision offered by Prowse's production. This was a play which was 'visually clear' but which nevertheless 'dismisse[d] the clichéd image of Webster as a dramatist of death and decay' (Billington 1996: 10). For Edwards, then, Webster is a poet of vice and corruption, rather than of death and decay; this is a more accurate characterisation of the dramatist than the Prowse-Eliot characterisation (on T. S. Eliot's view of Webster, see p. 60).

Again and again, critics commented on both the violence, and on the strong emotional responses enforced by that violence: 'some could not bear to look as characters clutched at the blood blossoming through their costumes' (Lapworth 1996). And many reviewers also deliberately juxtaposed contrasting tones and terminology, suggesting that a director and an audience receptive to Webster's aesthetic relativism had (whether fortuitously or not) encountered the text on something approaching its own terms: '*The White Devil* spells out a *gleefully savage* vision' (Murray 1996); 'Rightly, Miss Edwards sees the play also as an *appalling comedy*' (Murray 1996); 'Stephen Boxer as the Duke of Florence [. . .] is *fire and ice* in a manner one feels Webster originally intended' (Edmonds 1996) (italics mine). Allied to this was a sense that this was, indeed, a play which was resonant for the moment: 'Webster's imagery [. . .] comes across with startling clarity [. . .] especially the febrile coupling of sex and death that makes it so contemporary' (Edwardes 1996).

There were some mild voices of dissent raised: one critic thought that the 'social dimension' of the play was 'missing' (Peter 1996); another referred rather colloquially to Webster's 'warped and pervy imagination' (Spencer 1996; although this appears not to have been a criticism); a more measured respondent thought that 'Miss Edwards's production does not quite catch the right tone' (de Jongh 1996). By and large, though, audiences were only too willing to admit their delight in what they perceived as the play's (and the production's) 'gratuitous sex and violence [. . .] [which was] feverishly enjoyable' (Spencer 1996) and the 'gory special effects [. . .] Brachiano's death was particularly gruesome' (Schafer 1997: 119). It is possible, of course, to see this as the response of an audience which has become thoroughly desensitised to the spectacle of violence, and which perceives violence as a form of entertainment; but it is also possible to see it as a response which is closer to a Websterian vision of the world than has been possible at most times over the past four centuries. It may be that Webster is, indeed, our contemporary, and that directors like Noble and Edwards can help us to perceive this more clearly.

What is clear is that *The White Devil* reveals a concern with the relations between men and women, and this is something that Edwards' production sought to explore in detail. Much attention was paid in this production to 'the sneering, salivating Flamineo', and in particular his role of 'pimping for his married sister' (Coveney 1996: 13). Flamineo, the production suggested, was a crucial figure because he helped audiences to understand the gender roles which the play interrogated. The production placed particular emphasis on the limited roles available to women in this Renaissance society; and audiences were encouraged to think of the gender politics of their own time and place. So one critic thought that, through this production, 'Webster [. . .] emerges as a sharp-eyed analyst of male power structures' (Billington 1996: 10); another thought that the 'treatment of women in this play' was 'generally abominable' and that 'all the women are depicted as victims of male barbarity' (Spencer 1996). So 'even the very whole-some Marcello appeared to enjoy bashing and kicking Zanche' (Spencer 1996), and Vittoria and Isabella were presented as bearing the public guilt for Brachiano's sexual transgressions. But the production also emphasised the capacity of women to resist such acts of oppression; Teresa Banham gave an 'unusually vehement' portrayal of Isabella, for example, suggesting that the character is driven by 'a richly ambiguous mixture of altruism and anger' (Billington 1996: 10).

For the most part, however, the 'female resilience' which the production presented was always filtered through the lens of sexuality (Billington 1996: 10); 'for women the only lever avail-able to use against such men is sex', thought one reviewer (Hanks 1996). In fact, the production presented a sharply drawn portrait of both male and female sexuality, suggesting that sexual desire is both an energetically productive and catastrophically destruc-tive force. So Vittoria and Brachiano were linked by their sexual appetites, undertaking 'not so much a love-affair as a lust-affair, intensely and ruthlessly erotic' (Peter 1996). This was a production in which 'the stage seams with lust', where 'bodices are unlaced, bodkins bared and cod-pieces set a-quivering' (Coveney 1996: 13). Sexual desire informed the staging of all the set-pieces, including the trial of Vitttoria, where Monticelso 'peer[ed] surreptitiously down Vittoria's dress' (Billington 1996: 10), and 'circled hungrily around her, never actually touching her but slavering over her as if he longed to' (Schafer 1997: 119). If 'sex is both the play's driving force and the source of moral double standards' (Billington 1996: 10), then this production was very clear that Vittoria was the focus of much of the sexual desire represented on stage. Not only did Brachiano and Monticelso lust after her, so too did the 'always incestuous' Flamineo (Schafer 1997: 119):

> The incestuous element in the Flamineo/Vittoria relation-ship was extremely overt. Jane Gurnett [playing Vittoria] had her breasts manhandled as much by Flamineo as by Brachiano [. . .] When Richard McCabe's Flamineo wanted to threaten Vittoria at the end of the play, this included lasciviously licking as much of her skin as possible. (Schafer 1997: 119)

'Incestuous' was the word most frequently used to describe McCabe's interpretation of Flamineo (Spencer 1996; Billington 1996: 10).

As the focus of all this erotic attention, then, Jane Gurnett as Vittoria had the difficult task of presenting an interpretation of the character relevant to Webster's multifaceted presentation of the title role. She played Vittoria as a 'strongly sexual figure', driven by erotic energies as much as were the male characters (Billington 1996: 10). But those erotic energies could be restrained when needed and so in the trial scene Edwards and Gurnett presented the contrast between the male characters, driven by lust rather than by a quest for justice, and the 'defiant figure' of Vittoria (Spencer 1996), performing with 'monumental dignity' (Billington 1996: 10), and giving a physical sense of the 'isolation and entrapment' experienced by the character at this moment (Schafer 1997: 119). If the phrase 'isolation and entrapment' makes one think of the position of the Duchess of Malfi in Act Four of her play, that is perhaps because this *White Devil* was very much a companion of *The Duchess of Malfi*, in its emphasis on sibling incest, female sexuality and stoicism, and the interrogation of the link between restraint and desire. In its simultaneous stress on both the pleasure and the horror of sex and violence, it spoke to its late-twentieth-century audience in an emphatically contemporary voice.

CONCLUSION: RELATIVISM

What these productions suggest, then, is that contemporary theatre audiences have some degree of patience with the aesthetic relativism of Webster – the juxtaposition of laughter and horror in the 1980 *Duchess of Malfi* was easily understood by its audience – but resist the full-scale relativism of Webster's dramatic vision at its most extreme. Those productions which have been the most successful – Noble's *Duchess of Malfi* and Edwards's 1996 *White Devil* – have strived to contain their nods towards generic and tonal dislocation within an overarching 'consistent' interpretation of the play. It may be, indeed, that this is the only way that these plays can be satisfactorily staged in a contemporary theatre; it may even be, given the initial reaction to *The White Devil*, that this was the way in which the plays were most successfully staged under Renaissance theatrical conditions. Perhaps the full aesthetic relativism of Webster's vision awaits its practical realisation at some future point; perhaps it is simply too radical a conception of theatrical performance to make an audience feel anything other than disorientation and, perhaps, the slightest hint of horror.

NOTES

1. On the other hand, not every reviewer shared this opinion of McEwan; the critic for the *Times* thought, for example, that McEwan's 'oblique and quizzical style' presented Vittoria 'as an uninvolved comic spectator' (Wardle 1969).
2. See also Jane Edwardes' review in *Time Out*: 'When Brachiano removes his poisoned visor, the head that emerges looks as though it has been roasted overnight on a spit. It was enough to make one schoolgirl pass out at the final preview' (Edwardes 1996).

Appendix: Responses to Selected Major Productions of Webster's Plays

1945, *The Duchess of Malfi* (dir. George Rylands), Theatre Royal, Haymarket: 'The play opened at a time when the first reports and photographs of the survivors of the Nazi concentration camps were being published in the London newspapers, and in this context the critics discovered a seriousness and depth to Webster's purposes as never before' (Webster 1995: 433).

1947, *The White Devil* (dir. Michael Benthall), The Duchess Theatre, London: 'an impressive vindication of *The White Devil* as entertainment as well as tragedy' (Webster 1995: 109).

1960, *The Duchess of Malfi*, Shakespeare Memorial Company, London: 'powerful and intelligent' (Webster 1995: 435).

1965, *The White Devil* (dir. Jack Landau), Circle in the Square, New York: 'leaned towards a simplified gangster version of Webster' (Webster 1995: 110).

1967, *The Duchess of Malfi* (dir. Brian Shelton), Pitlochry Festival, Scotland: 'turned to Brechtian alienation as a modern theatrical mode that might do justice to the sententious and emblematic in Webster's style' (Webster 1995: 435).

1969, *The White Devil* (dir. Frank Dunlop), National Theatre, London: discussed in detail above.

1971, *The Duchess of Malfi* (dir. Peter Gill), Royal Court, London: 'played on a bare stage flanked by doors from a demolition yard [. . .] and with kitchen chairs and a table as props' (Webster 1995: 436).

1971, *The Duchess of Malfi* (dir. Jean Gascon), Stratford Shakespearean Festival, Ontario: 'atmospheric lighting, and eerily resonant music' (Webster 1995: 436).

1971, *The White Devil* (dir. Philip Prowse), Citizens Theatre, Glasgow: 'direction and design were again dominant' (Webster 1995: 111).

1975, *The White Devil* (dir. Philip Eyre), Playhouse, Nottingham: '[concerned with] the political dynamics of class and power' (Webster 1995: 112).

1976, *The White Devil* (dir. Michael Lindsay-Hogg), Old Vic, London: 'limited from the start both in conception and execution by the belief that Webster's thematic meaning could be surgically presented on the basis of plot alone, without the poetry and extensive vision of his language' (Webster 1995: 113).

1977, *The White Devil* (dir. Michael Blakemore), Guthrie Theatre, Minneapolis: 'the Vittoria, played as a Hollywood vamp, was criticized for lacking any emotional depth' (Webster 1995: 113).

1979, *The White Devil* (dir. Michael Kahn), Saratoga Springs, New York: 'one of the most misguided of modern productions [. . .] insensitive to verbal, intellectual, and dramatic values' (Webster 1995: 113).

1980, *The Duchess of Malfi* (dir. Adrian Noble), Royal Exchange, Manchester: discussed in detail above.

1983, *The White Devil* (dir. John McMurray), Bristol Old Vic, Theatre Royal: 'cool, deliberate approach [. . .] undercut the intellectual and sensual force of the conception and visual realization' (Webster 1995: 114).

1985, *The Duchess of Malfi* (dir. Philip Prowse), National Theatre, London: discussed in detail above.

1989, *The Duchess of Malfi* (dir. Bill Alexander), Royal Shakespeare Company: 'concentrated on emotional realism in acting, and [. . .] carefully avoided any hint of melodrama' (Webster 1995: 440).

1991, *The White Devil* (dir. Philip Prowse), National Theatre, London: 'all the principals seemed [. . .] subordinate to the director's vision of the atmosphere of the play' (Webster 1995: 115).

1996, *The White Devil* (dir. Gale Edwards), Royal Shakespeare Company: discussed in detail above.

1999, *The White Devil* (dir. Jason Byrne), Loose Cannon Theatre Company, Dublin: 'negotiated the Machivellian political and sexual intricacies of the first four acts with a rare precision' (Cave 2000).

2000, *The Duchess of Malfi* (dir. Gale Edwards), Barbican, London: 'fails to create a coherent world that can contain Webster's dark nihilism, oppositional faith and astonishing aphoristic poetry' (Billington 2000: 20).

2000, *The White Devil* (dir. Philip Franks), Lyric Theatre, Hammersmith: '[avoided] direct confrontation with Webster's radicalism' (Sato 2000: 104).

2003, *The Duchess of Malfi* (dir. Phyllida Lloyd), National Theatre, London: 'a world slowly infected by Ferdinand's madness' (Billington 2003: 22).

2006, *The Duchess of Malfi* (dir. Philip Franks), West Yorkshire Playhouse, Leeds: 'transposed the action from the 17th century to 1950s Italy with real flair' (Gardner 2006: 36).

Bibliography

Unless indicated otherwise, all references to Webster's plays are from Webster 1996.

Archer, Ian W. (1991), *The Pursuit of Stability: Social Relations in Elizabethan London*, Cambridge: Cambridge University Press.

Barber, John (1969), 'Triumph for Designer in Jacobean Tragedy', *The Daily Telegraph*, 14 November.

Barthes, Roland (1977), *Image-Music-Text*, London: Fontana.

Berry, Ralph (1972), *The Art of John Webster*, Oxford: Clarendon Press.

Billington, Michael (1995), 'What's it all about, Malfi?', *The Guardian*, 15 February, T4.

Billington, Michael (1996), 'Devilishly Good,' *The Guardian*, 29 April, p. 10.

Billington, Michael (2000), 'The Taming of *The Duchess of Malfi*,' *The Guardian*, 13 November, p. 20.

Billington, Michael (2003), '*The Duchess of Malfi*: National Theatre, London,' *The Guardian*, 29 January, p. 22.

Bliss, Lee (1983), *The World's Perspective: John Webster and the Jacobean Drama*, Brighton: The Harvester Press.

Bovilsky, Lara (2003), 'Black Beauties, White Devils: The English Italian in Milton and Webster,' *ELH*, 70, pp. 625–51.

Bradbrook, M. C. (1980), *John Webster: Citizen and Dramatist*, London: Weidenfeld and Nicolson.

Brooke, Rupert (1913), 'The Authorship of the Later *Appius and Virginia*,' *The Modern Language Review*, 8, pp. 433–53.

Brown, John Russell (1969), '[*The White Devil* as Tragedy],' in *John Webster: A Critical Anthology*, ed. G. K. Hunter and S. K. Hunter, Harmondsworth: Penguin, pp. 235–55.

Bryden, Ronald (1969), 'Swamped by Opulence,' *The Observer*, 16 November.

Carey, Katherine M. (2007), 'The Aesthetics of Immediacy and Hypermediation: The Dumb Shows in Webster's *The White Devil*,' *New Theatre Quarterly*, 23, pp. 73–80.

Carnegie, David, and MacDonald P. Jackson (2001), 'The Crux in *A Cure for a Cuckold*: A Cryptic Message, a Doubtful Intention, and Two Dearest Friends', *Modern Language Review*, 96, pp. 14–20.

Castle, Gregory (2007), *The Blackwell Guide to Literary Theory*, Oxford: Blackwell.

Cathcart, Charles (2006), 'John Marston, *The Malcontent*, and the King's Men', *The Review of English Studies*, 57, pp. 43–63.

Cave, Richard Allen (2000), '*The White Devil*.' *Research Opportunities in Renaissance Drama*, pp. 174–5.

Cecil, David (1969), 'John Webster,' in *John Webster: A Critical Anthology*, ed. G. K. Hunter and S. K. Hunter, Harmondsworth: Penguin, pp. 150–7.

Cinpoes, Nicoleta (2007), '*The White Devil* – Radio Productions', University of Warwick, http://www2.warwick.ac.uk/fac/arts/ren/ elizabethan_jacobean_drama/webster/white_devil/stage_history/ radio

Correll, Barbara (2007), 'Malvolio at Malfi: Managing Desire in Shakespeare and Webster', *Shakespeare Quarterly*, 58, pp. 65–92.

Coveney, Michael (1996), 'It's in the Blood', *The Observer*, 28 April 1996, p. 13.

Cropper, Martin (1985), 'Perverted Logic: *The Duchess of Malfi*, Lyttleton', *The Times*, 5 July 1985, p. 9.

Culhane, Peter (2004), 'The Date of Heywood and Webster's *Appius and Virginia*', *Notes and Queries*, 51, pp. 300–1.

Darley, George (1967), *The Life and Letters of George Darley Poet and Critic*, ed. Claude Colleer Abbott, Oxford: Clarendon Press.

De Jongh, Nicholas (1996), '*The White Devil*', *Evening Standard*, 29 April.

Dowd, Michelle M. (2003), 'Leaning Too Hard Upon the Pen: Suburb Wenches and City Wives in *Westward Ho*', *Medieval and Renaissance Drama in England*, 15, pp. 224–42.

Drake, Nathan (1817), *Shakespeare and his Times*, 2 vols, London.

Duffy, Eamon (1992), *The Stripping of the Altars: Traditional Religion in England, 1400–1580*, New Haven: Yale University Press.

Dunkley, Chris (1972), 'Historical Violence', *The Times*, 11 October, p. 11.

Dunlop, Frank (1969), *The White Devil: Programme Notes*, National Theatre, London.

Edmonds, Richard (1996), '*The White Devil*', *Birmingham Post*, 28 April.

Edwardes, Jane (1996), '*The White Devil*', *Time Out*, 1 May.

Ekeblad, Inga-Stina (1956), 'Storm Imagery in *Appius and Virginia*', *Notes and Queries*, 201, pp. 6–7.

Eliot, T. S. (1974), 'Whispers of Immortality', in *Collected Poems 1909–1962*, London: Faber, pp. 55–6.

Erne, Lukas (2003), *Shakespeare as Literary Dramatist*, Cambridge: Cambridge University Press.

Foucault, Michel (2003), 'What is an Author?' in *The Essential Foucault: Selections from Essential Works of Foucault, 1954–1984*, ed. Paul Rabinow and Nikolas Rose, New York: New Press, pp. 239–53.

Gabel, John Butler (1969), 'The Dates of Chapman's *Conspiracy and Tragedy of Byron*', *Modern Philology*, 66, pp. 330–2.

Gardner, Lyn (2006), 'The Sweet Smell of Villainy and Deceit', *The Guardian*, 30 October, p. 36.

Gray, David Henry (1927), '*Appius and Virginia*: By Webster and Heywood', *Studies in Philology*, 24, pp. 275–89.

Greg, W. W. (1926), 'Some Notes on Ben Jonson's Works', *The Review of English Studies*, 2, pp. 129–45.

Gunby, David (2004), 'John Webster (1578x80–1638?)', *The Oxford Dictionary of National Biography*, Oxford University Press, http://www.oxforddnb.com/view/article/28943

Gurr, Andrew (2004), *Playgoing in Shakespeare's London*, 3rd edn, Cambridge: Cambridge University Press.

Hanks, Robert (1996), '*The White Devil*, The Swan, Stratford', *The Independent*, 29 April 1996.

Hazlitt, William (1821), *Lectures on the Dramatic Literature of the Age of Elizabeth*, London: John Warren.

Henslowe, Philip (2002), *Henslowe's Diary*, ed. R. A. Foakes, 2nd edn, Cambridge: Cambridge University Press.

Hirsch, Brett D. (2005), 'An Italian Werewolf in London: Lycanthropy and *The Duchess of Malfi*', *Early Modern Literary Studies*, 11.

Hunter, G. K. (1969), 'From "English Folly and Italian Vice: John

Webster"', in *John Webster: A Critical Anthology*, ed. G. K. Hunter and S. K. Hunter, Harmondsworth: Penguin, pp. 256–83.

Hunter, G. K. and S. K. Hunter, eds (1969), *John Webster: A Critical Anthology*, Harmondsworth: Penguin.

Ioppolo, Grace (2006), *Dramatists and their Manuscripts in the age of Shakespeare, Jonson, Middleton and Heywood: Authorship, Authority and the Playhouse*, London: Routledge.

Jack, Ian (1969), 'The Case of John Webster', in *John Webster: A Critical Anthology*, ed. G. K. Hunter and S. K. Hunter, Harmondsworth: Penguin, pp. 157–64.

Jackson, Ken (2003), 'Bethlem and Bridewell in the *Honest Whore* Plays', *Studies in English Literature 1500–1900*, 43, pp. 395–413.

Jackson, MacDonald P. (2001), 'Late Webster and his Collaborators: How Many Playwrights Wrote *A Cure for a Cuckold?*' *Papers of the Bibliographical Society of America*, 95, pp. 295–313.

King, Andrew (2004), 'Sheppard, Samuel (c.1624–1655?)', *The Oxford Dictionary of National Biography*, Oxford University Press, http://www.oxforddnb.com/view/article/25347

Kingsley, Charles (1873), *Plays and Puritans: and Other Historical Essays*, London: Macmillan.

Lamb, Charles (1808), *Specimens of English Dramatic Poets, who lived about the time of Shakespeare; with notes*, London: Longman.

Lapworth, Paul (1996), 'The Theme-Park of Death', *Stratford Herald*, 2 May 1996.

McLuskie, Kathleen and Jennifer Uglow, eds (1989), *Plays in Performance: The Duchess of Malfi, by John Webster*, Bristol: Bristol Classical Press.

Marcus, Frank (1969), '*The White Devil*', *The Sunday Telegraph*, 16 November.

Marston, John (1997), *The Malcontent and Other Plays*, ed. Keith Sturgess, Oxford: Oxford University Press.

Masten, Jeffrey (1997), *Textual Intercourse: Collaboration, Authorship, and Sexualities in Renaissance Drama*, Cambridge: Cambridge University Press.

Maxwell, Baldwin (1944), 'The Source of the Principal Plot of *The Fair Maid of the Inn*', *Modern Language Notes*, 59, pp. 122–7.

Montaigne, Michel de (1603), *The Essayes*, translated by John Florio, London.

Moore, Don D., ed. (1981), *John Webster: The Critical Heritage*, London: Routledge.

Morgan-Russell, Simon (1999), '"No Good Thing Ever Comes Out Of It": Male Expectation and Female Alliance in Dekker and Webster's *Westward Ho*', in *Maids and Mistresses, Cousins and Queens: Women's Alliances in Early Modern England*, ed. Susan Frye and Karen Robertson, Oxford: Oxford University Press, pp. 70–84.

Murray, David (1996), 'Mixed Signals from the RSC', *Financial Times*, 29 April.

Oliphant, E. H. C. (1911), 'Problems of Authorship in Elizabethan Dramatic Literature', *Modern Philology*, 8, pp. 411–59.

Ornstein, Robert (1961), 'The Dates of Chapman's Tragedies, Once More', *Modern Philology*, 59, pp. 61–4.

Pearson, Jacqueline (1980), *Tragedy and Tragicomedy in the Plays of John Webster*, Manchester: Manchester University Press.

Peter, John (1996), 'Two for the Road?' *The Sunday Times*, 5 May.

Plutarch (1579), *The Lives of the Noble Grecians and Romans*, translated by Thomas North, London.

Price, Hereward T. (1969), 'The Function of Imagery in Webster,' in *John Webster: A Critical Anthology*, ed. G. K. Hunter and S. K. Hunter, Harmondsworth: Penguin, pp. 176–202.

Ray, Sid (2007), '"So Troubled with the Mother": The Politics of Pregnancy in *The Duchess of Malfi*,' in *Performing Maternity in Early Modern England*, ed. Kathryn M. Moncreif and Kathryn R. McPherson, Aldershot: Ashgate, pp. 17–28.

Saintsbury, George (1911), *A History of English Criticism: being the English chapters of A History of Criticism and Literary Taste in Europe, revised, adapted, and supplemented*, Edinburgh and London: Blackwood.

Sato, Mika (2000), '*The White Devil*', *Research Opportunities in Renaissance Drama*, pp. 103–4.

Schafer, Elizabeth (1997), '*The White Devil*', *Research Opportunities in Renaissance Drama*, pp. 117–19.

Schwartz, Elias (1959), 'The Dates and Order of Chapman's Tragedies', *Modern Philology*, 57, pp. 80–2.

Sidney, Sir Philip (2006), 'The Defense of Poesy,' in *The Norton Anthology of English Literature, Volume 1*, ed. Stephen Greenblatt et al., New York: Norton.

Smith, A. J. (1970), 'The Power of *The White Devil*', in *John Webster*, ed. Brian Morris, London: Ernest Benn, pp. 71–91.

Smith, James (1969), 'The Tragedy of Blood', in *John Webster:*

A Critical Anthology, ed. G. K. Hunter and S. K. Hunter, Harmondsworth: Penguin, pp. 116–32.

Spencer, Charles (1996), 'Illuminations in a Dark Universe', *The Daily Telegraph*, 29 April 1996.

Sullivan, Garrett A. Jr. (2005), *Memory and Forgetting in English Renaissance Drama: Shakespeare, Marlowe, Webster*, Cambridge: Cambridge University Press.

Wall, Wendy (2006), 'Just a Spoonful of Sugar: Syrup and Domesticity in Early Modern England', *Modern Philology*, 104, pp. 149–72.

Webster, John (1830), *The Works of John Webster*, ed. Alexander Dyce, 4 vols, London.

Webster, John (1995), *The Works of John Webster: An Old-Spelling Critical Edition, Volume One*, ed. David Gunby, David Carnegie, Antony Hammond and Doreen DelVecchio, Cambridge: Cambridge University Press.

Webster, John (1996), *The Duchess of Malfi and Other Plays*, ed. René Weis, Oxford: Oxford University Press.

Webster, John (2003), *The Works of John Webster: An Old-Spelling Critical Edition, Volume Two*, ed. David Gunby, David Carnegie and MacDonald P. Jackson, Cambridge: Cambridge University Press.

Webster, John (2007), *The Works of John Webster: An Old-Spelling Critical Edition, Volume Three*, ed. David Gunby, David Carnegie and MacDonald P. Jackson, Cambridge: Cambridge University Press.

Weil, Judith (1999), '*The White Devil* and Old Wives' Tales', *The Modern Language Review*, 94, pp. 328–40.

Wiggins, Martin (1997), 'Conjuring the Ghosts of *The White Devil*', *The Review of English Studies*, 48, pp. 448–70.

Williamson, Elizabeth (2007), 'The Domestication of Religious Objects in *The White Devil*', *SEL: Studies in English Literature 1500–1900*, 47, pp. 473–90.

Index